TWO *for* THE MONEY

TWO *for* THE MONEY

THE SENSIBLE PLAN FOR MAKING IT ALL WORK

JONATHAN AND **DAVID MURRAY**

with Max Alexander

CARROLL & GRAF PUBLISHERS
NEW YORK

TWO FOR THE MONEY
The Sensible Plan for Making It All Work

Carroll & Graf Publishers
An Imprint of Avalon Publishing Group, Inc.
245 West 17th Street
11th Floor
New York, NY 10011

AVALON
publishing group incorporated

Copyright © 2006 by David Murray and Jonathan Murray

First Carroll & Graf edition 2006

Library of Congress Cataloging-in-Publication Data is available.

ISBN-13: 978-0-78671-787-3
ISBN-10: 0-78671-787-4

9 8 7 6 5 4 3 2 1
Interior design by Sue Canavan
Additional research by Nate Hardcastle
Printed in the United States of America
Distributed by Publishers Group West

FOR JANET AND JENNY—TO DEDICATE THIS BOOK TO YOU
HAS BEEN, BY FAR, THE EASIEST DECISION
WE'VE HAD TO MAKE

CONTENTS

Acknowledgments

We'd like to thank our families for their encouragement and support. Our wives and our children (Jonathan, Kate, and Grace, Palmer, and Luke) *all* showed remarkable patience and understanding throughout this process. You are the best children we could ever ask for, and we are proud of each of you for separate, interesting, and wonderful reasons. To our wonderful mom (Brenda), our dad (Boyd), and Emily: as a family of five, we learned growing up together that family is what it's all about . . . especially when you're eating Vincent's Pizza. You make it easy to look back at our lives with joy. To The PrivateBank (David) and to Jed, Dave, Gregg, Brigid, and Jason (Jonathan): thank you for the support and flexibility you provided. Thanks also to Warner, John, and Jay for their advice over the years.

We'd like to gratefully acknowledge our clients, especially those who agreed to interview for the book. Your testimonies make these sometimes-murky financial issues identifiable and embraceable for others; and by sharing your experiences, you will help many.

And finally, we owe so much to Max Alexander (our partner-in-writing), Will Balliett (publisher), the phenomenal team at Carroll & Graf, and Jonathan Pecarsky (William Morris). To set forth on a project like this is exciting; that we finished it happily together is a tribute to your professionalism and kindness.

Preface

Life was a lot simpler when we were growing up. Our own childhood in suburban Pittsburgh in the 1960s would look familiar to lots of baby boomers. We played baseball, earned merit badges in the Boy Scouts, and rode our bikes everywhere. On warm summer nights, we played with our neighborhood friends until our mothers shouted for us to come in (no cell phones then!). We took piano lessons, did chores on Saturday mornings, and went to public high school with kids who had two basic choices after graduation: get a well-paying union job in a factory, or go to college and possibly earn a bit more.

As in most families then, our dad worked and our mom stayed home; they met in junior high and have been together since. Both sets of our grandparents lived nearby, and were very involved in our lives. Vacations meant driving to a lake—not flying to some tropical island resort and spa. Our house was small by today's standards, although it seemed plenty big for the five of us at the time. Dad wore the same handful of ties for years. Our cars were always used, but they got us from point A to point B. More often than not, they even started on cold winter mornings.

Those were very good times. We were taught that what we had was good enough—and better than most in the world. "Our family is lucky for a lot of reasons," Dad used to say, "but mostly because we have each other."

Money was never discussed in front of us—except our own money, which had to be earned. At age eight we started doing yard work, picking up sticks and raking leaves for small change. Four years later we had the biggest paper route in the area. The Sunday morning *Pittsburgh Press* was the size of a phone book, so Dad would pile us into the station wagon—he'd be wearing his robe and slippers—and drive us along the route. On freezing winter mornings it would still be dark, of course, the headlights of our faux-paneled Country Squire lighting our way as we dashed up yet-to-be-shoveled front walks.

The commitment Dad made to us was inspiring, and even then it included primary lessons in working hard, maintaining a positive attitude, and being smart with your money. We both had passbook savings accounts for our newspaper earnings, and we loved to watch the money grow and earn interest.

Later on, we started doing more serious yard work and snow shoveling around the neighborhood for spare cash—a job that grew into a full-scale landscaping business by high school.

At college, we pursued separate interests. David majored in geology and lived independently with a tight group of non-fraternity guys. Jonathan majored in English literature, joined Theta Chi, and became a resident advisor. But we had plenty of time together, having formed an acoustic act (inspired by Crosby, Stills, and Nash, of course) that even developed a little following at local clubs and coffeehouses.

But most of our college work was less glamorous. One

summer we were janitors at a high-rise apartment complex, where we spent two full months stripping twenty years of wax from dingy linoleum corridors. Another summer we toiled for ten bucks an hour (big money at the time) in a stuffy office, encoding reams of old legal documents onto computers as part of a lawsuit against Gulf Oil. It was awful. The highlight of the work day was the forty-five-minute lunch break at Burger King! Those two jobs convinced us how important it is to find work that you enjoy. (And that one person's deadly dull job is another's oasis; there are no absolutes when it comes to career choice.)

Today we both work as financial advisors. David is Managing Director of Wealth Management for The PrivateBank in Bloomfield Hills, Michigan. Jonathan is a senior vice president of investments in the Baltimore office of a major New York Stock Exchange firm. We also appear regularly on NBC's *Today* show and CNBC, where we cover the financial issues facing baby boomers—their retirement dreams, their kids, their aging parents.

We share the same basic values, not to mention the same shoe size, but we are hardly clones. David embraces change, has moved nine times in the past twenty years, and is more independent, more organized, and also more introspective; he's likely to favor a somewhat conservative investment philosophy.

Jonathan, in David's words, is "the nice one." He's more easy-going and settled—he's been in the same home for fifteen years—and he's consistently cheerful, less prone to worry, and very social. Financially speaking, he leans toward prudent risk.

And just as no twins are truly the same, there is no "one-size-fits-all" financial plan. Throughout *Two for the Money*, we'll cover the financial challenges that face our generation—more than 78 million in the United States alone. We'll share helpful insights that other boomers have provided. And along the way, we'll challenge each other, and you, to go beyond pat formulas and to *think differently* about your money and your life—so you can make the best decisions for yourself and the people you love.

In this hectic and competitive wireless world, it can seem as if we never have the time to stop and take a breath. We certainly don't remember our parents multitasking at this rate. So maybe it is inevitable that as we've gotten older (and, we hope, wiser) both of us are seeing life more as a call to ourselves than as a race against others. Defining our own game of life, and succeeding at that, is, finally, our greatest goal, and in essence, the subject of this book.

Introduction

If we listed all of the financial questions we've heard over the past twenty years—on *The Today Show*, CNBC, and our radio call-in show, as well as from our own clients—three would stand out above the rest:

1. Will I have enough money to retire?
2. How can I pay for my children's education?
3. Will I be able to take care of my parents?

We hear these questions virtually every day. More and more Americans—especially the 78 million born during the "baby boom" from 1946 to 1964—are growing increasingly anxious about their family's future. Someone even coined a term: the Sandwich Generation—an apt metaphor for us, as we are caught between our kids' wants and our parents' needs, while simultaneously dealing with our own busy lives. And as boomers shoulder these important challenges, many tell us that they yearn to maximize the last third of their lives. Especially upon turning fifty, people tell us: "I want to spend more time with my family," "I want to see the world," "I'd like to make a difference," "I want to do something meaningful . . . something fulfilling."

And the odd thing is that people don't really talk to each other about this stuff—like it's taboo. When we were kids, *Mad* magazine ran a feature that employed "thought balloons" to show what people were *really* thinking. Here's the grown-up version:

What the world sees boomers doing:	What boomers are really thinking:
Shopping at the mall.	My credit card is maxed out.
Talking to the boss on the cell phone.	I wish I could afford a job in the nonprofit sector.
Driving an SUV.	Mom shouldn't be driving.
Working out on the Stairmaster.	Dad can't climb the stairs anymore.
Taking a daughter to dance practice.	She wants to go to Juilliard and we budgeted for state college.
Buying a six-burner dual-fuel Viking range.	Mom made good food on her Amana.
Eating squab confit at an overpriced restaurant.	Why don't we stay home and cook on one of the six burners?
Adding a master bedroom suite.	Should we sell the house now, before the bubble bursts?
Charging a spa vacation.	Mud bath will be free when we're homeless.
Working twelve-hour days.	Dad worked less, saved more.
Christmas in Europe.	Why does Mom's nursing home cost more than a London hotel?
Planning cruise vacations in retirement.	We're sinking.

It's not easy living a dual life—and there's no reason you should have to. But with a sensible, realistic, one-day-at-a-time approach, *Two for the Money* will help you successfully navigate the unique financial *and* emotional concerns so many of us are faced with.

Boomers are often accused of being selfish, especially when compared to our parents. Born after the war and raised in prosperity, the "Me Generation" took a lot for granted, and demanded still more. In the sixties and seventies, we rebelled against authority, grew our hair, and railed against materialism. Twenty years later, we returned to the suburbs, where we built homes that our parents could never have imagined. Along the way, boomers became the most marketed-to and self-absorbed generation in history—thanks in large part to the electronic mirror of television, which reflected our own lives every night after dinner.

Not surprisingly, boomers have a label for everything. Now we're calling ourselves the Sandwich Generation.

Many people, including our own mother, understandably ask what all the fuss is about. "Every generation since the beginning of time has dealt with kids and parents!" Mom observes. And she's right. So what make our generation so different?

It's a good question. Here are five good answers:

- **College was not a necessity for previous generations**, when relatively well-paying union jobs could be had right out of high school. Our kids, by contrast, are unlikely to attain basic middle-class security, let alone affluence, without a college degree—the cost of which is vastly outpacing inflation and wage growth.

- **Our parents are living longer**, thanks to new drugs and treatments, but at great cost. The average monthly bill for a nursing home is over $5,000. Assisted living costs $4,000 a month on average. And that doesn't include prescription drugs or hospital stays.

- **We had children later in life.** Many of us waited to have kids until our careers were in gear. Women are having children in their forties nowadays. Unlike previous generations, we're facing college costs and elder parent care at the same time.

- **Our families are smaller and more dispersed.** Postwar families were generally smaller than previous generations, so many of us have fewer siblings to bear the burden of parental care. Our siblings also are more likely to be dispersed; long-distance caregiving is time-consuming and expensive.

- **Retirement today lasts longer and is more expensive.** In fact, retirees today should expect to spend as much time in retirement as they did in the workforce.

If that isn't enough, consider this:

A baby boomer turns fifty every eight seconds. That's more than 10,000 fiftieth birthday celebrations per day.

Leave It To Beaver was a long time ago. For many boomers, the time to make a plan is here. This book will help you get started today on a path to financial security. First, some basic math:

$$\$85,000 + \$120,000 = \$1,002,571$$

Does that seem a little fuzzy? Not when you factor in the incredible power of compounding. Here's how it works: let's say you're fifty years old and have just $85,000 in your 401(k) retirement plan. You know it's not nearly enough, but you're in good company, because $61,000 is the national average balance in 401(k) plans as of December 2005. But it can easily become enough. *If you start now, putting just $250 per paycheck ($500 per month) into that account would yield over $1 million at age seventy,* based on the historic annualized stock market return of 10%. That's right—by adding a mere $6,000 a year for twenty years, you could retire a millionaire. That's the power of investing. If your portfolio averages 8 percent per year, your remaining balance would be $713,288. Compound at 12 percent, and you'd have $1,420,495 in the bank. Naturally, since you're investing in stocks, returns could be higher or lower.

Incidentally, some may suggest that it's unrealistic to expect a 12 percent annual return from stocks. We disagree. It's *inadvisable*, but quite realistic—as long as you stay invested for at least twenty years. In the next chapter we discuss this further, but for now, you may be heartened to know that 12.32% is the median annual rate of return on the S&P 500 stock index over the fifty-nine rolling twenty-year periods between 1928 and 2005.

In fact, if you plug in the investing parameters we described above, in forty-one of fifty-nine periods your ending balance would have exceeded $1 million. That's 69 percent of the time! Now having said that, don't *expect* to earn 12 percent per year from stocks. Shoot for an average return of 8 to 10 percent per year over meaningful periods of time, with lots of accompanying bumps along the way. What we earn from stocks is not the point here. The point is, it's not too late!

In this book, we'll share stories and challenges from real people—people with issues that may be similar to yours. So if you're wrestling with any of these issues, know that you're not alone.

We'll introduce you to Mary, a married mother of two and part-time employee in the billing department of a local medical group. She struggles with the challenges of taking care of her family and making ends meet;

there is an increasing amount of friction in her marriage when the subject of money comes up. Credit cards are a big culprit.

You'll meet Richard, a senior advertising executive working sixty hours a week. He's forty-six, married, has three college-bound boys, and an elderly mother recovering from hip replacement surgery. He wonders about his life, and where the time has gone.

Then there's Dennis, who recently became a member of the "Fired at Fifty" club—too young to retire, too old to hire. At his age, debt is not the problem. He simply doesn't have enough savings to retire.

We'll show you how we helped each of these folks, and invite you to join us as we share ways to tackle the often complex world of finance, money, and investing.

Sometimes it seems like personal financial advice is about as reliable as that Magic 8 Ball toy we all used to shake and study. *Two For the Money* will cut through the mystery to give you effective solutions, valuable resources, and tools you can use for years to come. When we advise clients, we ask them to think of us as their financial coaches. We'll do the same for you. Here's what you can expect:

First we give you the basics:

- determining how much money you need;
- getting organized;
- building a budget, getting out of debt, and developing a strategy for saving;
- understanding investing.

Then, we zero in on you and your money:

- redefining your retirement;
- making your money work more effectively;
- talking to your spouse about money;
- dealing with unexpected challenges;
- understanding wills, trusts, and insurance.

Finally we cover your kids and your parents:

- teaching younger kids about money, and teenagers about spending, savings, and credit;
- paying for your children's education;
- coping with your kids after college;
- talking with your elders about their money (and yours);
- long-term care insurance and living arrangements;
- health care options.

Throughout the book you'll find **Double Takes**, in which David and Jonathan take sides on subjects on which we have differing points of view. Double Takes recognize that there is often more than one good solution to a problem.

In addition, boxed features called **Tools for the Money** will drill down into a specific topic for more detailed instructions. Think of Tools as favorite and time-tested recipes that get handed down in your family; they'll always work for you.

Now that we've given you the sound-bite version of the book, it's time to roll up your sleeves. Remember, your concerns are shared by millions of other people, including us. So on every page, you're never alone.

Chapter One:

How Much Is Enough?

$1,000,000

Remember Dr. Evil in *Austin Powers*? The clueless arch-criminal from the sixties is brought back to life in the nineties, where he threatens to destroy the entire civilized world—unless he is paid the breathtaking sum of . . . "One *million* dollars!" Everybody laughs, of course, because a million isn't what it used to be. The fact is, $1 million is more or less the minimum that an average American couple without a pension needs for a secure—but average—retirement.

Only about 2 million Americans are millionaires. But as we have already demonstrated in our introduction, saving just $250 per paycheck, on top of an $85,000 401(k), can yield $1 million after twenty years, based on the average return of the Standard & Poor's (S&P) 500 since 1929.

Still, it's understandable that $1 million seems out of reach to anyone struggling to pay bills and keep a head above water. You might be thinking, "A million dollars? I'll tell you what: pay off my credit cards and give me $100,000 in the bank, and I'll be happy! Who needs to retire a millionaire?"

The reason is simple: *When you are retired, the paychecks stop coming.*

That might seem obvious, but it's worth thinking about because lots of people ignore that fact until retirement is almost upon them. Here's a valuable lesson we've learned from retirees: a paycheck is like fuel for your gas tank. As long as you keep putting the gas in, you can drive pretty much wherever you'd like, knowing that you'll be filling her up every two weeks. When you retire, however, you have only *one tank of fuel remaining* (your life's savings) . . . and as you would with the "last chance for gas" fill-up before crossing the Mojave Desert, you'd better make it last! Ask any first-year retiree and they'll tell you: it can be uncomfortable adjusting to a world without paychecks.

The other related problem (though it's actually good news) is that you are likely to live a long, long time in retirement. The average American retiring at age sixty-five can now expect to live eighteen more years. That's nearly one-fourth of his entire life with no paychecks. For a sixty-five-year-old couple, one member has a 50 percent chance of living to ninety-two!

But perhaps we're exaggerating. What about Social Security? Surely that will cover at least *some* of the expenses. It's true that today Social Security is paying an average annual benefit of $18,000 to a married worker retiring at age sixty-five. (For a more precise calculation of your own benefits, go to www.ssa.gov/OACT/quickcalc.) The future of government-sponsored retirement benefits is anybody's guess, but it's unlikely that they'll rise (beyond inflation adjustments) or get cut back drastically. It is highly likely, however, that future benefits will start at a later age—say, seventy.

Keep in mind that Social Security is *not* a pension plan, and was never meant to be. It's an insurance policy with a large risk pool (the whole country) designed to prevent old-age poverty. So even assuming you stay in good health, Social Security will not maintain your current lifestyle and will probably not even come close to replacing your current paycheck. (Interestingly, the children of boomers have already given up on *their* Social Security. One survey showed that more Americans under age forty believe in UFOs than in future Social Security benefits.)

Maybe you have a solid pension that guarantees 80 percent of your income for life, along with lifetime health care benefits. If so, congratulations! Between your pension and Social Security, you probably can get by without much in savings, assuming you stay in relatively good health. But pensioners are in an exclusive club, and one that's shrinking: according to the nonprofit Employee Benefit Research Institute (EBRI), just 20 percent of American workers now have so-called defined-benefit pension plans—down from 39 percent in 1975. (By the way, the federal

Calculating Retirement Savings

To get a fix on how much money is enough for your retirement, start by identifying how much annual income (in today's dollars) you will need. (Figure on at least 70 percent of your current income, but preferably 100 percent. For the purposes of this exercise, we're pretending Social Security doesn't exist—which it may not!)

Write that number here: _____

You'll need to generate your required annual income by withdrawing an average of 5 percent annually from your nest egg. So the formula is:

Annual Income ÷ .05 = Retirement Money Needed

For example, if you need $50,000 in annual retirement income, the formula would be $50,000 ÷ .05 = $1 million.

Write that number here: _____

Once you identify how much money is enough for retirement, it's not hard to calculate how much you should be saving every month to reach that goal. Figure you'll be investing in growth stock funds that spin off a 10 percent annual return over the long run. Factor in a 4 percent inflation bite, and you're realizing actual growth of 6 percent. Assuming you plan to retire at age sixty-five, multiply your retirement fund by one of the following factors to determine your monthly savings. (You can get figures for any retirement age or amount on Web-based calculators, such as those at www.choosetosave.org/calculators.)

Current age	Factor
25	.000500
30	.000699
35	.000991
40	.001436
45	.002154
50	.003422
55	.006072
60	.014262

For example, if you are currently age forty and need $1 million to retire at age sixty-five, the formula would be $1 million x .001436 = $1,436 per month in savings.

Write your monthly savings here: _____

Pension Benefit Guaranty Corporation, which insures pension plans when companies go belly-up, is billions of dollars in the red and sinking because so many companies have made pension promises they can't keep. That doesn't include the huge public pension bill—for teachers, cops, bureaucrats at every level of government—that is guaranteed by taxpayers.)

Like it or not, for most of us retirement has become a do-it-yourself project.

Apparently, many of us think it's a *weekend* project. According to EBRI, four in ten workers currently are not saving anything for retirement. And even those who do save are not saving nearly enough—possibly because they don't know better. One study found that 42 percent of boomers have no idea how much they'll need for retirement. And two-thirds of Americans over thirty are clueless as to what their monthly budget should be in retirement.

It shouldn't be such a mystery. In fact, it isn't. One focus of economists' attention has been determining how much you can withdraw from your investments without burning through the principal before you die. That's pretty important when the paychecks stop coming and your investments are all you've got. We explain the details in a sidebar (see the Tools for the Money section on "Rolling the Monte Carlo Dice" on p. 16), but for now it's enough to know that a conservative investment advisor might recommend safely withdrawing about 4 percent annually; a more aggressive investor might be okay with 6 percent or more. Our actual advice would take into account the age of the client and the recent performance of the market, but a reasonable average—for the sake of argument—would be 5 percent.

Now let's go back to our million-dollar retirement fund. We can see that a 5 percent annual withdrawal equals $50,000, or about $4,000 a month. Can you live on that? No doubt many can—with ease. Others will say no way, and many are probably not sure. One common mistake in retirement planning is to assume you'll need less money than your current income. We don't always agree on that, but, at the very least, you should plan for 70 percent or 80 percent of your income—and that presumes good health.

But enough blackboard economics for the moment. Rather than calculate percentages, we think it's more useful to actually *imagine* your retirement. Visualize it! By starting at the end point and getting a handle on where you want to be, you will bring your financial needs into focus. To get you thinking about life after the retirement party, we created four typical retirement scenarios, ranging from basic to lavish. We were thinking of that classic song by George Jones and Tammy Wynette called "We're Not the Jet Set (We're the Old Chevrolet Set)." Whether you drive a Chevy to the general store or jet off to Gstaad for the holidays, you need a retirement plan that fits your lifestyle. Of course, no two people are alike (even twins), but it's possible that your retirement looks something like one of these scenarios (see pages 8 and 9). Keep in mind that the numbers are in today's dollars, and that they assume you'll also be receiving Social Security benefits.

One thing you can see right off the bat is that a million bucks

A very basic retirement	An average retirement
You're happy in a very small house, with low utility bills and no mortgage.	You currently enjoy a typical middle-class lifestyle, and you want to maintain it in retirement.
You live, or plan to live, in a community with a low tax rate.	The house you own now is just fine, needs no renovations, and will be paid off by retirement.
You enjoy preparing and even growing your own food; restaurant meals are a waste of money to you.	A dinner out and a movie once a week, or every other week, is plenty of entertainment.
You're happy driving older cars.	You plan to take infrequent vacations, and time them to take advantage of off-season rates.
You take occasional vacations by car, and you stay in budget hotels.	You're happy spending time with grandchildren, who live nearby.
You shop for clothes only when you need something.	When you read magazines, you don't long for the stuff in the ads.
You have no club or membership dues.	You like simple hobbies such as gardening, walking, fishing, and reading.
You will have no debt of any kind, including car loans or leases.	You have no credit card or automotive debt.
You would consider part-time work.	You're willing and able to work part-time if property taxes or health care costs increase during retirement.
Cost: $500-$2,000 per month **Retirement Funds Needed:** **$150,000-$500,000**	**Cost: $2,000-$8,000 per month** **Retirement Funds Needed:** **$500,000-$2 million**

A very comfortable retirement	A lavish retirement
You want to retire in a resort community, such as a beach or golf development.	You want (or already own) a large home in a very expensive area.
Or you want to retire in a big city and enjoy cosmopolitan amenities such as theater and professional sports.	Utility bills on your home will total $1,000 or more a month.
You plan to join a gym or other club.	You will own more than one home.
Your home or condo will probably be paid for, but high taxes and association fees are likely.	You plan to eat lunch and dinner mostly in restaurants and clubs.
You plan to have nice furniture and new appliances.	You drive expensive cars, and buy new cars every few years.
You enjoy restaurant meals two or three times a week, especially at new places in town.	You'll belong to several clubs and have season tickets to sports and cultural events.
You hope to take at least one "memorable" vacation in season per year, such as Europe in the summer or the Caribbean in the winter.	You plan on taking many luxury vacations, staying in four-star hotels.
You'll need a good-sized closet full of nice clothes to wear when you're out and about.	You spend $1,000 or more a month on clothes.
Social activities are important, and you plan to entertain often.	When you thumb through magazines, you can definitely see yourself buying the stuff in the ads.
Cost: $8,000-$50,000 per month **Retirement Funds Needed:** **$2 million-$10 million**	**Cost: $50,000-$100,000 per month.** **Retirement Funds Needed:** **$10 million and up.**

won't do it for many of you. Do you yearn for a very comfortable retirement? Get saving! Even if you see yourself as the average guy next door, the high end of that average retirement will take more than a million.

On the other hand, average retirees really *can* get by on less than $1 million in retirement. We actually know lots of them. They live frugally and simply, which is not a bad way to go. One of our favorite people is our uncle, Tim Palmer, who is not yet retired but lives a simple life that most people would envy. When we were growing up, Tim worked as a county planner in central Pennsylvania. His job required a lot of communication skills— helping people to understand how land use and environmental decisions made today would affect their community long into the future. "It was a great job," Tim recalls, "but the fundamental problem was that many people didn't believe there was a problem. They couldn't see what was happening to their place because the changes happen so gradually. Because of that, I got interested in communicating better with people, which led me to writing."

After seven years on the job, at age thirty-two, Tim decided that his true calling was writing books about the natural environment. He quit his county job, loaded up his van, and headed West. "At the time, it was scary," he says. "I had a little bit of money invested, but not much. So I became quite proficient at minimizing my needs. For twenty-two years I essentially lived out of my van, collecting stories and writing books."

Tim, who's now fifty-eight, went on to publish seventeen

books—and counting. One of his latest, *Pacific High: Adventures in the Coast Ranges from Baja to Alaska*, chronicles his nine-month journey from Mexico to Kodiak Island. When he's not writing, Tim travels the country delivering talks and slide shows on environmental issues.

He doesn't live in his van anymore. In fact, Tim and his wife, Ann Vileisis, also a writer, own a charming 1,200-square-foot home that's half a block from the ocean in Oregon. (They have no children.) And when we say they own it, we mean it—as in, no mortgage. "I am totally allergic to debt," Tim says. He avoids debt by frugal living. "I finally replaced my old van when it had 180,000 miles," he says with pride. "We wear our clothes out." Tim has to think hard when asked to name something he recently spent money on. "Let's see, I just bought a new backpack; the old one was twenty-six years old."

For Uncle Tim, life after retirement will look pretty much like life before retirement. "The things I'm passionate about are backpacking in the wilderness, skiing in the backcountry, whitewater rafting, and spending time with my wife and friends," he says. "You don't have to pay a lot of money for those things. My emphasis is on experience rather than accumulation. I would not want most of the stuff that comes with a larger paycheck."

In the next chapter, we'll talk about how frugal living is a sure path to financial security, even a path to riches. But we know that many people do want more than the basics in their retirement. And here's the really important thing: *having more money gives you more choices.* Our dad always told us, "Money is freedom." So if backpacking really does end up being the love of your life for thirty years of retirement, great! But if your knees give out in year ten, then what? Well, if you've saved enough money, you can decide that sailing is your true calling and ship out.

HEDGING AGAINST INFLATION

More money is also the best hedge we know against inflation. And *inflation is the enemy of your retirement security.* During your working life, inflation pressure is muted. The rising cost of everything from groceries to cars to real estate is tempered by the fact that you receive salary or wage increases along the way—probably not as much as you'd like, but the system generally works; if it didn't, no one could afford to buy anything, and prices (and inflation) would drop according to the laws of supply and demand. Presently, the Consumer Price Index (CPI) is roughly 3.5 percent. Many components of the index however, are inflating at double or triple that rate. The fact that prices rise is proof, if you will, that the average person is earning enough to buy (or is willing to buy on credit, a problem we'll talk about in Chapter Three). Some economists even argue that a little inflation is a good thing for the average worker, who benefits from rising wages over time.

By contrast, our retired clients tell us that inflation is never good news for them. They don't call it inflation; they call it "the cost to live." If the "cost to live" looks like this:

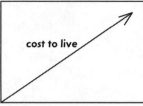

and your income stream looks like this:

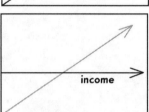

at some point in time, when those lines intersect, bad things will happen to you. That's why it's crucial for retirees to have an income stream—built from their investments—that goes up like this:

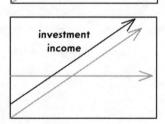

When you're retired, your only protection against inflation is from the return on your investments. And a skimpy investment portfolio might not generate enough gain to keep up with inflation. Here's where the mystery comes in: nobody can predict future inflation. But we *can* look at averages. Since 1914, the average annual inflation rate has been 3.49 percent.

(An aside: The highest annual inflation rate in the United States was 17.80 percent in 1917, reflecting wartime debt, and the lowest was negative 10.85 percent—that's called deflation— in 1921. In the latter case, rising unemployment coupled with a

(continued on p. 18)

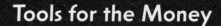

A Better Way to Look at Historic Stock Market Returns

If you were to go all the way back to 1928 and dissect the S&P 500 into rolling twenty-year periods, there would be fifty-nine of them (1928-1947, 1929-1948, etc.). The average annual rate of return over those periods was approximately 12 percent. At that rate, your money doubles every six years. (Remember the "rule of seventy-two" from Economics 101, which teaches that a rate of return divided into seventy-two reveals how many years it will take for your money to double.) Over that "median" twenty-year period, a $100,000 investment grew to $948,542! The best twenty-year period occurred from 1980-1999, when investors earned an eye-popping 17.83 percent per year on their money. During that fortuitous twenty-year span, your $100,000 investment (including dividends reinvested)

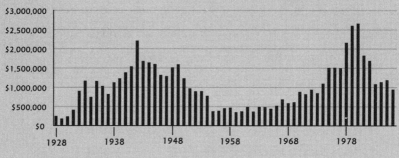

20-Year Periods of S&P 500 Index

Ending value, after 20 years, of a $100,000 initial investment with quarterly dividends reinvested (by year invested)

(year of initial investment)

Source: Thomson Financial

grew to a whopping $2,660,912. No wonder investor Warren Buffett once said the best time to sell stock is never.

The worst twenty-year period for stocks occurred from 1929 to 1948—no surprise as it included the Crash of '29, the Great Depression, and World War II. Average annual return during that period was 3.09 percent. ($100,000 grew to $183,000.)

Here's an overview of the results from those periods:

- Two twenty-year periods doubled your money.
- Five tripled it, seven quadrupled it, and two quintupled it.
- In two periods, your $100,000 grew to more than $600,000.
- In two more, it grew to more than $700,000.
- Five periods saw growth to more than $800,000, and five grew to more than $900,000.
- *In twenty-eight of the rolling twenty-year periods (47 percent of the time), $100,000 grew to more than $1 million: a tenfold increase in twenty years.* And in four of those periods, you'd have more than $2 million.
- In *none* of the twenty-year periods would you have lost money.

Rolling the Monte Carlo Dice

To get a handle on those worst-case scenarios, economists employ a risk analysis tool called the Monte Carlo method. Essentially, it's an algorithm that automates statistical sampling through the use of a computer. (Statistics junkies can purchase Monte Carlo software for Excel called Crystal Ball at www.crystalball.com.)

The Monte Carlo concept was developed by the Polish-born mathematician Stanislaw Ulam, who worked on the atomic Manhattan Project during World War II and later invented the hydrogen bomb with Edward Teller. During a long illness in 1946, Ulam occupied himself playing solitaire and began to ponder how many ways existed to win (or lose) at the Canfield variation. Ulam later recalled, "After spending a lot of time trying to estimate them by pure combinatorial calculations, I wondered whether a more practical method than 'abstract thinking' might not be to lay it out, say, 100 times and simply observe and count the number of successful plays." (This was already possible to envisage with the beginning of the new era of fast computers.)

It's not a perfect system. For one thing, Monte Carlo simulations don't reflect that portfolio performance depends on future returns, which no one can predict, rather than past performance. And they don't take into account the various asset classes that a real stock portfolio would have; everything is random, which is not the way real people allocate their investments. Finally, Monte Carlo simulations assume an investor will stick it out, even in a bear market; that is often not the case.

Those caveats aside, Monte Carlo simulations can help us understand, and avoid, worst-case scenarios. For example, projections show that withdrawing 8 percent annually from a stock fund can sometimes be very bad for your health. How bad? During nine twenty-year periods of withdrawing 8 percent annually from the S&P 500, you ended up with less than your original $1 million at the end of the game. During eight more twenty-year periods, *you lost everything . . . ran out of money . . . died broke.* In other words, in seventeen out of fifty-nine periods of taking out 8 percent a year, you ended up with *less principal than you started with.* That's 30 percent of the time. There are circumstances in which we'll take those odds—but not with our life savings.

So the point is, yes, stocks have been a proven way to build wealth over time. A fully invested portfolio of stocks is an excellent way to grow your money. But if you have income needs (the way retirees do), and you're thinking about taking money out of stocks, you'd better be extremely careful about *when* and *how much* you withdraw. During a bear market, even withdrawing 4 percent annually can be risky especially if you have retired recently and you need that money to last for decades.

In a bull market, we'd recommend limiting withdrawals to 6 percent or 7 percent. If you're looking for a simple back-of-the-envelope number to use for a withdrawal program (from a good blue-chip stock fund), plug in 5 percent. Normally, if stocks continue to average 8-12 percent per year returns, you should be okay. Be sure to talk to your financial advisor, however. Your situation may warrant a more cautious approach.

notoriously obstinate Federal Reserve that refused to lower interest rates led to plunging prices, since no one could afford to buy anything. That's supply and demand for you. That year beat the worst deflation in the Great Depression, which clocked in at negative 10.30 percent in 1932. The worst *inflation* in our own time was not in the much-maligned 1970s but actually in 1980, when it peaked at 13.58 percent. The prime rate in 1980 hit 20 percent! For more fascinating historic and current information on inflation, go to www.inflationdata.com.)

Often, people see that inflation has been "tamed" at about 3.5 percent over time and they get a warm, fuzzy feeling. Hasn't the Federal Reserve Bank "cured" runaway inflation? Is this really an issue in your retirement planning?

Definitely.

For starters, economies can develop minds of their own and sometimes don't respond to manipulation by the Fed. Double-digit inflation could happen again. But never mind that; the bigger issue is plain-vanilla inflation, which really adds up over time. Over the entire 20th century, inflation reduced the value of a dollar to a nickel. Many people are surprised when we tell them that, after twenty years, annual inflation of just 3.5 percent will *double* the cost of living.

Here's another concern: In 1999, changes in how the government calculates the Consumer Price Index (CPI) reduced the size of the resulting inflation increases. As a result, we believe the CPI is now underreflecting the true cost for retirees. To be safe,

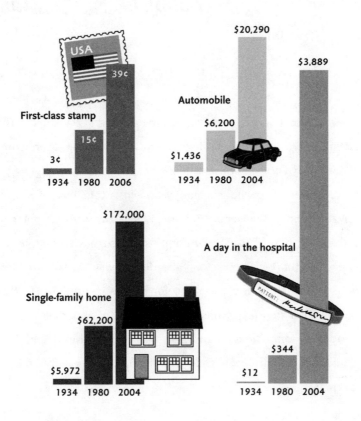

$20,290

$3,889

First-class stamp

Automobile

39¢

15¢

$6,200

3¢

$1,436

1934   1980   2006

1934   1980   2004

$172,000

A day in the hospital

Single-family home

$62,200

$344

$5,972

$12

1934   1980   2004

1934   1980   2004

Source: First-class stamp: Postal Rate Commission; all the other data: *The Wall Street Journal*, January 3, 2006

retirees should assume annual inflation of 5 percent. At that rate, someone retiring at age fifty-five with $5,000 per month in annual expenses will need *four times* that amount by age eighty-five.

Inflation is a primary enemy of your retirement, but other factors also influence how much money you need to maintain your chosen lifestyle.

How Much Is Enough for College?

The rising cost of college makes health care look like a bargain. The latest report from the College Board (www.collegeboard.com) shows 2005-2006 tuition and fees at a public university grew 7.1 percent over the previous school year, with a total cost of $5,491. Private, nonprofit university tuition and fees advanced 5.9 percent, with a total cost of $29,026. Another study suggested that, in ten years, the total cost of a four-year degree will hit $140,000 for public universities and $300,000 for private institutions. At that rate, two children (say, twins like us) would set back their parents $600,000—*after taxes*. Translated, that means Mom and Dad would have to earn more than $1 million, just to pay for college. Ouch.

David: Saving for your kids' college is great if you have the money, but it should not be your number-one priority. There are many ways to get financial aid for college—about $129 billion is available annually—but there is no such thing as a retirement scholarship or loan. You need to keep your eyes on *that* prize, then worry about college. Plus, if you save and invest enough for your retirement, chances are good you'll leave your kids a legacy that will pay for *their* kids' college.

While we're at it, don't obsess over getting your kid into Harvard. Studies show that those exclusive Ivy League degrees may not buy happiness, and don't necessarily give grads a leg up careerwise. Chances are your child may be just as likely to succeed and be happy with a degree from a good state university. It's what the student puts into it and gets out of it that matters, not where she goes.

And don't forget that kids can help pay their own way through college. One idea gaining favor is that kids take a year off after high school. Many experts complain that college has become a high-pressure and obligatory career mill; a year off is like pressing the "reset" button. It also gives you and your child time to sock away extra cash.

I don't believe college tuitions will keep up their recent double-digit annual increases, because the law of supply and demand won't allow it. More than $1 million in earnings to send two kids to a private college? Come on. If that becomes true, only the ultra-wealthy will be able to afford college, and nobody wants that. Something's gotta give.

Jonathan: Wow, Dave, what college did *you* go to? Didn't I go there, too? While I agree that college saving should be a lower priority than retirement saving, I can't counsel ignoring it completely. It's the elephant in the room for most families, and with skyrocketing costs you need a plan. I'd budget $100,000 per kid for college, and that's just for a public university.

(continued on next page)

(from previous page)

As a former assistant dean of admissions, I know that most schools do try to separate merit from finances. Ideally, they want the best and brightest students, regardless of their ability to pay. The decision to grant or deny admission used to be totally separate from the decision to provide financial aid. In those days, many colleges were able to boast, "We meet 100 percent of the financial need of our students." They no longer say that. Unfortunately, I've seen that wall start to crumble as rising costs make it harder for schools to ignore a family's financial situation. More often than you might expect, the ability to pay has entered into the admission equation. Not that admissions officers come out and ask if a student has the bucks—but if the school's development director just happens to mention that Johnny's dad is the CEO of the Acme Global Corporation, well, that could be considered. You don't want to be in the position of turning down an acceptance to your kid's first-choice school because you can't foot the bill. So start saving (and see Chapter Nine)!

THE LONGEVITY EQUATION

"How long will I live?" If only we could answer that question! It would make retirement planning so easy. Plug in the number of years and the funds needed per year, build in some inflation protection, and voila!—one foolproof retirement package. Unfortunately, the rub is that no one really knows how long the money has to last. All we can do, of course, is base our planning on average life expectancies. But this is one of the most misunderstood aspects of retirement. When you consider that most people would rather not think about their own death, it's strange how many of us *underestimate* how long we will live. The reason is that life expectancy for any individual is a moving target. For example, if you were born in 1950, your life expectancy *at birth* was 68.2 years. (That's an average of men and women, and all races; one good source for details on life expectancy is www.info-please.com.) But that figure takes into account that many people will die young—in car accidents, or military service, or job injuries, to say nothing of fatal illnesses that can strike at any age.

But once you get to age fifty-five, many possible causes of death have been eliminated or reduced. You probably don't drive as fast as you did at age twenty, you're not likely to die in war, and so on. In other words, once you've made it that far, there's a good chance you'll live way beyond your at-birth life expectancy. Right now, an American man in good health who makes it to age sixty-five has a 50 percent chance of living to age eighty-five. He has a 25 percent chance of making it all the way to ninety-two. For a woman, the corresponding figures are even higher. She can expect a 50 percent chance of living to eighty-eight, and a 25 percent chance of making it to ninety-four. So the odds are good that you'll be around in retirement for a long, long time—perhaps even *forty years*.

Age	Life Expectancy	Years out of the workforce (if retiring at 65)
65	83	18
70	85	15
75	86.5	21.5
80	89	24

Source: National Center for Health Statistics, National Vital Statistics Report, Vol. 53, No. 6

That's a long time to go without a paycheck, and another reason why you need more for retirement than you might think.

FACTORING IN GOOD HEALTH

Modern medicine is why Americans are living longer in retirement. Yet, paradoxically, medical care can be one of the costliest drains on retirees. We talked about 3.5 percent average inflation. Health care costs break that mold. In 2001, they rose 8.1 percent, totaling 14 percent of the nation's gross domestic product.

In 2003, health care consumed 10.3 percent of pretax income for seniors aged sixty-five to seventy-four, and 15.1 percent of pretax income for folks seventy-five and older. That's a huge chunk of retirement funds! It's estimated that a sixty-five-year-old couple retiring now will burn through $190,000 in health care costs during their retirement—above and beyond Medicare benefits.

What that figure does *not* take into account is the cost of assisted living or nursing-home care. If you're currently helping parents with long-term care issues, you already know how expensive that can be. The costs vary widely across the country, so it's impossible to generalize. Assisted living, a relatively new concept geared to retirees who need help with daily activities but don't require the intensive medical care of a traditional nursing home, can run $10,000 to $75,000 annually, depending on where you live and the level of service you need. Nursing homes cost more—from $45,000 to $125,000 annually—but also qualify for Medicare, which may pay for some of the cost. The best way to prepare for the possibility of assisted living or a nursing home is to buy long-term care insurance, starting at about age fifty-five. (Buying it sooner exposes you to the risk that you'll die before you need it; buying it later will cost more.) The best way to prepare for the overall cost of retirement health care is to plan for high medical bills when you calculate your retirement savings.

Bottom line: If you want a number to shoot for, $1 million will buy a healthy couple a modest retirement. But if inflation spikes

or your health deteriorates, you could run out of money—
especially if your portfolio hits a land mine, like the 2001-2002
bear market. A considerably more secure retirement can be
funded with $2 million, spinning off a six-figure income and
protecting you against inflation and medical costs. If you are not
there yet, read on. The rest of this book will help you get there.

Chapter Two:

Getting Organized

All problems become smaller if you don't dodge them but confront them. Touch a thistle timidly and it pricks you; grasp it boldly and its spines crumble.

—Admiral William F. Halsey, Jr.

When we had our landscaping business in high school, a big job every spring was preparing garden beds for the new season. We would spend hours pulling weeds, turning soil, and adding mulch. This was not the romantic part of gardening; the covers of seed catalogs never show an exhausted laborer bent with a shovel over a manure pile. But as every gardener knows, the spade work is essential if new seeds are to grow and thrive. A freshly prepared garden bed doesn't dazzle like a May floral display, but there's an inner beauty—literally—to those neat rows, and a great feeling of pride knowing the seeds are off to a good start.

It's the same way with your financial "garden." Taking care of the fundamentals will pay off down the road. It can be scary to open that shoebox filled with your bills and tax receipts and vow to make sense of it all, but the alternative is more frightening. A lot of people go through life feeling like they have no control over their money—a money market account here, a checking account there (the balance is a mystery), a few old 401(k) plans from jobs you quit years ago, maybe a savings bond your uncle gave you, way too many credit and store cards, and a bunch of bills that always seem to be overdue.

Getting your financial life in order is about more than having a neat place to pay bills, although that's an excellent start—if you can't see your finances under the clutter, how can you manage them? The bigger picture is about taking control of where your money goes. It's about understanding your expenses, eliminating debt, and planning for the future. Some of this is psychological. People who take charge of their money feel as though they are in control of their lives. By being proactive, not reactive, with your money, you are *empowering yourself to be wealthy*. And make no mistake about it: rich people don't get that way by spending money. They are goal-oriented, pay their bills on time, do not run credit card balances, and avoid risky debt. On the other hand, people who are careless with their finances and constantly borrow money will always be poor and will never reach their goals, no matter how much stuff they acquire.

In this chapter, we'll walk you through all the steps to financial organization, starting with your mailbox and ending with your computer. You'll learn how to:

- Organize your bills and statements so nothing ever gets lost.
- Balance your checkbook, twenty-first-century style.
- Shift to automatic!
- Create an emergency contact sheet.

The rest of the book flows from the good habits you'll learn right here. You have to get this stuff right in order to be able to save for your retirement, or pay for your kids' college, or help your parents find the right elder care. If you are already a neatnik, can locate your current electric bill in the dark, have no debt, and are saving 15 percent of your take-home pay on top of your maxed-out 401(k), skip this chapter. The rest of you (everyone raise their hand!) can read on.

MAIL CALL

For many people, the shoebox under the desk overflowing with papers constitutes financial planning. You've heard the phrase "messy desk, messy mind." Allow us to elaborate: *the less desk you can see, the less money you'll have.* That's because when you subscribe to the single-pile method of money management, important things inevitably get lost. And when you misplace bills, forget about payments, and lose tax-deductible receipts, you will, sooner or later, lose money. Trust us on this.

So . . . how much is it worth to you to get organized?

Think of it this way. The Internal Revenue Service is *very* organized. They almost never lose track of a taxpayer, dead or alive. Your cable company is *even more organized* (except when the cable guy says he'll be there between eight and ten). In fact, in the history of cable television, going back to the Dark Ages when HBO was still called Home Box Office, your cable company has never lost a check. (This can be proven, we think.) We could go on and on. When was the last time a restaurant made a mistake on your bill? (Okay, a mistake in your favor.) Not very often, huh? How many times has Steve Jobs sent you two iPods instead of the one you ordered? Dream on. The point is, all of the nice folks to whom you are shelling out your hard-earned cash are very organized. If you're to stand a ghost of a chance at keeping some of that money for yourself, you need to be just as organized.

In the world of finance, like the world of your closets, the enemy of organization is clutter. Clutter comes in many forms, but lots of it enters your house through the mailbox—that pile of catalogs and credit card offers mixed in with the important bills and statements.

1. Toss the junk.

There are all sorts of ways to combat clutter, but all share one common characteristic: immediacy. That is, people who manage to keep clutter at bay waste no time when clutter arrives. As a matter of fact, most of the successful people we know tend to be "seize-the-day" types who deal with issues as soon as they cross their path. Here's one proven technique: the minute you pick up your mail, pitch all the catalogs you don't need into the bin. Did you receive two identical mailings from the California Kelp Company? Immediately call the company's toll-free number and cancel one of them. (If you already have enough kelp to last a lifetime, cancel both.) Marketers use all sorts of gimmicks to convince you their junk mail is URGENT! and REQUIRES YOUR IMMEDIATE ATTENTION!—from envelopes that look like tax refund checks to phony Post-it notes from your boss.

Then move on to the credit card offers—except that these should get run through the shredder. You don't have a paper shredder? Then you really should go down to your local office supply store and buy one; a light-duty home model costs about $20. Twenty bucks! It's sad to say, but plenty of people have nothing better to do than paw through your trash at the dump, looking for credit card numbers and other sensitive information so they can steal your identity. Once they target you, it can be very time-consuming—which means costly—to clear your name. Twenty bucks.

2. Save the bills.

What's left in your mail after catalogs and junk are bills, statements, and checks. Okay, bills and statements, and maybe a birthday card from your mother. Here again, dealing with bills and statements requires immediate action. (Calling your mother to thank her for the card isn't a bad idea, either.) Leaving important financial documents in a pile on the dining room table does not constitute a system. But systems can be very simple. One good plan is to file bills in a special basket or large envelope (you can even tape the envelope to the side of your computer monitor). Then pay them all once a month; some people like to pay their bills once a week. Either way, keep them in one safe place. Once you pay a bill, file it away. We like those accordion files that have twelve pockets, one for each month. At the end of a year, you can toss last January's bills and start again with this year's.

3. Store the statements.

Bank statements can go in the same basket or envelope, because you should make it a habit to balance your checkbook whenever you pay bills—at least once a month. Once you've checked your ATM slips against the statement (keep those slips all together in one place, too), you can shred them. Should your bank still send you canceled checks (most don't anymore), you can also shred those once they're reconciled against the statement, unless you think you might need one as proof of some major purchase.

Pitch Perfect
(When to Toss Paperwork)

Auld Lang Syne: Things to *shred* (not throw out!) once a year:
- Monthly bank statements
- Monthly brokerage account statements (save the annual statement for four years)
- Annual Social Security statement (it comes two months before your birthday; replace the old one with the new one)

Things to keep for a while:
- Home improvement records and receipts (until you sell the house and have satisfied capital-gains tax laws)
- Warranties (until they expire or you sell the thing)
- Tax returns (for at least six years; forever won't hurt)

Things to keep in a bank safe-deposit box because you would need them after a fire destroyed your home:
- Property deeds
- Car titles
- Original birth certificates
- Wills and trusts
- Receipts for major purchases like pianos and boats, for insurance purposes
- A videotape documenting all your belongings

KEEP YOUR BALANCE

Many people equate checkbook balancing with root canal. Their anxiety stems from the often justified fear that they have spent more than they earned, and that balancing will reveal the terrible truth. The other anxiety is the process itself—reconciling checks, ATM receipts, and deposit slips, then trying to find that $5.80 discrepancy. Once you get organized, these fears will fade away.

1. Watch out for pricey mistakes.

These days, balancing your checkbook is more important than ever. That's because banks don't discourage overdrafts anymore—they use them to wring more revenue out of customers through a device they call "courtesy overdraft protection."

This checking account feature allows banks to honor checks, debit-card purchases, or ATM withdrawals that exceed your account balance—and for that "courtesy" they'll charge between $20 and $35 per overdrawn transaction, plus a $2 to $5 fee for every day your account is in the red. The bank usually won't alert you when your balance goes negative, and you'll rack up those fees on every subsequent transaction until you get your balance back in the black. Those charges add up to big money: the Center for Responsible Lending, a consumer watchdog group in Durham,

North Carolina, reports that account-holders now pay $10 *billion* per year in overdraft penalties.

Many consumers first learn about this "protection" when they receive bank statements laced with hundreds of dollars in fees. Don't let that happen to you: ask your banker whether your account carries this service and whether you can refuse it. And, whatever you do, keep your checkbook in balance.

2. Shift to automatic.

If you're like us, you probably don't write many actual checks anymore. Just about everyone we know uses a debit or credit card to buy stuff, including groceries, and then pays bills online. In fact, you can save money by setting up your bills to be automatically deducted from your checking account.

For example, many lenders will reduce your mortgage rate by a quarter point just for agreeing to have the monthly payment deducted automatically. If you think that's chump change, guess again: say you're borrowing $200,000 at 7 percent annual interest for thirty years. Setting up automatic deduction lowers your rate to 6.75 percent, resulting in a savings of $33.40 per month. If you invested that $33.40 in the stock market every month, after thirty years you would have earned $75,500.29, assuming the S&P average of 10 percent annual return. And you thought money didn't grow on trees!

What's more, automatic bill paying can be a lifesaver for the elderly. Setting it up for your parents can help them live independently, and put your mind at ease in the process.

While you're at it, consider setting up an automatic savings plan. Mutual fund companies do this every day. Simply call your advisor or fund company and tell them you'd like to set up an automatic investing plan. They'll tell you what they need—usually a voided check from your bank, with some paperwork to complete—and you'll be set up. No checks to write, envelopes to find, or stamps to buy. Every month, on the day of your choice, your bank will wire funds into your mutual fund(s). Clients tell us that they don't even miss the money. And you can sleep well, knowing that a portion of your savings is now on autopilot!

3. Use your computer.

Online banking can be done right on your bank's Web site, or you can do it through the Web site of a money-management software program like Intuit's Quicken or Microsoft Money. These programs, which cost about $30 for a basic version, are really great. Just ask Sarah, a forty-seven-year-old teacher and mother in Maine, who uses Quicken to balance her family's checkbook:

> *I used to balance our checkbook manually every month, but as we got older and our assets and expenses grew, it*

became so unwieldy—reconciling all those debit card slips. Now, as long as I'm careful to enter everything in regularly and accurately, the program automatically balances the checkbook, usually to the penny. That almost never happened in the past! At first, I was a little scared to use it because I'm not really a computer geek; I was worried I'd have to take a class or pore over some tutorial, but it's completely intuitive. I like that the interface looks like a traditional checkbook register.

At tax time, it's really easy to add up categories. One click tells you how much you spent on medical bills, or office supplies, for the year or any other time period you want. You can also keep track of expenses and monitor your budget, although I don't do that as often as I should. I wouldn't recommend buying the more expensive deluxe versions that include investment tools, unless you really plan to use them. For me, it's really about the check balancing and tax help.

If I had to name a caution, I'd say you just need to be careful to enter in all of your paper records like bills and checks; that part of it is still manual, and if you forget to do it, no software can save you. I find it a real time-saver to enter my financial transactions at the end of each day. That keeps it from becoming a big, burdensome job if you wait to do it, say, every two weeks or so when you typically pay your bills. Also, be sure to plan your expense categories carefully, and stick to them. Having a hundred items listed under "Miscellaneous" doesn't really help at tax time. You need to know exactly what you spent your money on.

CREATE AN
EMERGENCY CONTACT SHEET

Even if you're organized, automated, and computer-literate, the unexpected can happen. Time after time, when we meet with clients who have experienced a family emergency, they describe how difficult it can be, emotionally and physically. Part of the stress has to do with all of the challenges associated with finances and money, insurance, wills, government forms, account numbers, and key contacts. We'll discuss this further in Chapter Eight, but meanwhile you'll want to create a simple file that includes all of your important financial information. It doesn't have to be fancy. Be sure to include account numbers, passwords, and names and numbers of advisors and attorneys. Keep a copy in your safe deposit box, and give a copy to a close relative or a trusted friend. If and when you need it, you (or your spouse) will know exactly where to go.

Chapter Three:

Build a Budget, Find the Free Money, and Get Out of Debt

DON'T BREAK THE BUDGET

Making a budget (by hand or using the same kind of software program that balances Sarah's checkbook in the last chapter) should be your very next organizational goal once you're paying bills on time and balancing your checkbook.

We can hear you groaning, but don't despair: a budget, like exercise, becomes habit-forming and makes you healthier—and you don't have to keep track of every penny you spend (at least not forever). Here's how to do it.

1. List your expenses.

First, make a list of all your annual expenditures. Spend some time on this step; go through your checkbook, and try to think of everything. Don't just look at one month, because some bills, like car insurance, are paid every few months. (Money management software really helps here.) Be careful in how you categorize, separating needs from wants and the necessary from the frivolous. So "home repair" is not the same as voluntary "home improvement," which should be a separate category. Do not call "credit cards" an expense! Instead, break out what you spend on dining, entertainment, gifts, and so on. For now, if you take out cash from your bank as "walking around money," just call it "cash" or "allowance." But don't lump groceries in with cash.

Average Annual Expenditures

	Boomers (45-54)	National Average
Entertainment	$2,407	$2,060
Household furnishings and equipment	$1,801	$1,497
Apparel and services	$1,953	$1,640
Food away from home	$2,688	$2,211
Food at home	$3,693	$3,129
Fruits and vegetables	$621	$535
Alcoholic beverages	$477	$391
Telephone services	$1,156	$956

Source: Bureau of Labor Statistics, Consumer Expenditure Survey, 2003

2. Calculate your monthly expenses.

Divide the amount under each category by twelve to reflect your monthly expenses. Thus you will have a monthly entry for car insurance, even if you only pay it twice a year. The same goes for car repair bills, which can be unpredictable in the short term but are guaranteed to happen sooner or later; you might as well plan for them. Add up all the monthly expenses.

3. Add up your monthly income.

Now calculate your family's monthly take-home pay. If you or your spouse gets paid once or twice a month, that will be easy. If you get paid every two weeks, multiply your paycheck by 2.17, which is how many two-week periods are in each month, on average.

4. Do the math.

Here's where it gets exciting. Compare your monthly take-home pay to your monthly expenses. If your expenses exceed your income, don't jump off a bridge; most people new to budgeting spend more than they earn, thanks to credit cards. Budgets make that clear, and put you on a road to recovery. Go back into your budget and refine your categories. List all fixed expenses that would be difficult to cut back on, such as your mortgage payment, life insurance premiums, utility bills, car repairs, and medical expenses, and set them aside for the moment. (Cable TV is *not* a utility, but cable Internet might be considered one, especially if you do much work at home.) The remainder of your expenses will be in categories where there is clearly wiggle room—like gifts, dining, entertainment, and so on.

FIND THE FREE MONEY

What do we mean by free money? We mean identifying items in your budget that are not strictly necessary, then cutting them back. This is not as scary as it sounds; in many cases, you'll find you spend money on things that are really wasteful, if not downright silly. Cutting them out is like finding free money. (If you spend more than you earn, the only other option is working harder to earn more money—and that is definitely *not* free.)

So start taking whacks at your variable expenses, cutting back here and there, to try to get your expense number lower than your income number. You might have to make several passes, but be realistic. Don't just cut something in half that you know you can't live without. If the budget is unworkable, it won't work.

Having said that, you will have to make a few tough choices. Here are some of our favorite ways to cut back and still enjoy life.

1. Eat at home.

Until fairly recently, families in Italy ate out almost every night at lively neighborhood *trattorie*. Groceries in Italy were expensive, and the restaurants were relatively cheap, so it made sense. But those days are over, and not just in Italy. Competition among large supermarket and discount chains has made groceries in western nations almost sinfully cheap. (If you want to see really cheap food, go to Wal-Mart, but you probably already knew that; Wal-Mart is now America's largest grocery chain.) Meanwhile, restaurant prices have soared, in part due to labor costs. It takes a lot of bodies to make and serve all that food; that's one reason why even high-end restaurants have notoriously low profit margins. (Unless you really know what you're doing, do not open a restaurant. Restaurants are the Bermuda Triangle of small businesses.)

Some people spend vast portions of their take-home pay at restaurants—not just the fancy dinners, but all the little stuff that adds up: a bagel and coffee in the morning, a sandwich from the deli for lunch, a snack in the afternoon. If you live within your means, save regularly for retirement, and budget responsibly for all those meals out—bon appetit! But if you open the credit card statements at the end of the month and groan, then you need to go on a restaurant diet.

Try not to think of eating dinner at home as punishment. Buy a few candles, use cloth napkins, and put on some music. Start simply, by making easy one-dish meals; cookbooks on this subject abound. If you work too late to cook, try making soups and casseroles in advance on the weekend. (An electric slow cooker is great for this.) You might find yourself actually enjoying cooking, and getting more adventurous on weekends. Soon you will probably learn what all accomplished home cooks know: restaurant meals are mostly about theater; good food can be whipped up easily and far more cheaply at home. Make it a party and invite some friends over. For the cost of a bottle of wine in a fancy restaurant (typically three times what you'd pay at retail), you can serve an impressive meal for four people.

2. Drive older cars, for longer.

You really pay through the nose for that new-car smell. As soon as you drive that baby off the lot, it's officially used—and worth a lot less. Most cars lose 60 percent of their value in the first four years. Rather than lament that fact of life, you can capitalize on it. Let someone else pay for the new car; then you can buy it a few years later and save a ton of money. This wasn't such a good strategy for our parents' generation, when cars weren't built nearly as well. (We remember our dad on cold winter mornings, desperately trying to breathe life into the Country Squire wagon.) Today, however, reliable models can easily last ten years without any major headaches. You can buy a late-model car after year three and still get seven years' use—maybe more, if you drive less than the national average of about 12,000 miles annually.

The car industry has made it easier for you to do this, thanks to the proliferation of leases. Leasing a car is generally a bad idea; it's the most expensive way to buy a car because you essentially finance the whole thing. You don't even know the actual interest rate, because it's technically a rental and doesn't fall under truth-in-lending laws, but you can assume the rate is high. So let the other guy lease a new car for two or three years, after which it

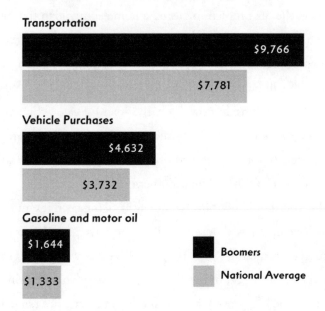

Average annual transportation expenditures

Transportation
$9,766
$7,781

Vehicle Purchases
$4,632
$3,732

Gasoline and motor oil
$1,644
$1,333

Boomers

National Average

Source: Bureau of Labor Statistics, Consumer Expenditure Survey, 2003

ends up back on the dealer's lot—ready for you to buy at a bargain. Most leased cars are in excellent condition and typically still have good warranties. Some even smell almost new.

While we're on the subject of cars and financing, be careful about car loans. The major car manufacturers actually make more money selling loans than they do on the cars themselves; not surprisingly, they are more than happy to load you up with debt while you're being dazzled in the showroom. Even good car loans have higher interest rates than mortgages or home equity loans, and the interest is not tax deductible. (You should always shop around for a car loan; it's amazing how fast the dealer's rate will drop when he knows you've checked at your bank.) Some people beat the tax problem by using a home equity loan to buy a car. But it's not wise to gamble your home's equity on a car, which depreciates in value over time. There is always the danger that you will still be paying off the loan after the car has fizzled. (It's called being "upside down" on the loan.) That's why you should never take out a car loan for more than four years; three is even better. If you can only afford that car with a seven-year loan, then you can't afford the car—period.

Ideally, you should not borrow money at all for a car. It's much better to save up a few thousand dollars and buy an old but reliable clunker—something with 100,000 miles that will get you to work and back for a year or two. (*Consumer Reports*' annual spring car-buying issue lists proven, reliable models in every price range.) Then take the money you would have spent on car payments and save it for a better car. Keep trading up like that, and after a few years you will "graduate" to nice cars, and you'll always have enough money in the bank to pay cash. Rich people *always* pay cash for cars—so start buying rich already!

3. Rent the DVD.

Have you ever wondered why so many people line up to see a movie on the first weekend it opens? You can go to the exact same movie a week later, and there's no line (and no tall guy sitting in front of you). Most grown-up movies—dramas, romantic comedies—look and sound fine on today's high-quality TV sets. The window of time between a film's theatrical and DVD release has shrunk to just four months; if you can wait that long for at least some movies, you and your spouse can save a bundle on entertainment and eat better popcorn—at a fraction of the price—in the process.

How much can you save? Well, according to the Bureau of Labor Statistics, the average American household spends $2,060 a year on entertainment. That's more than it spends on clothing or education, and nearly as much as on health care! The figure includes home-based entertainment like cable TV—another area where you can often cut back, just by eliminating expensive premium channels. Besides, didn't your parents tell you that TV would rot your brain? Try budgeting just $1,000 a year on entertainment—half the national average. That's roughly enough for expanded basic cable, plus one theatrical movie and three rented DVDs per month. The extra thousand you save can go into a college fund for your kids.

4. Avoid short-term fashions.

This applies to everything from clothes to kitchen counters. The concept of "fashion" was invented to get people to buy more stuff more often than they would otherwise need. After all, most clothes will last several years; why, if not for "fashion," would you need to replace your wardrobe every year? We mentioned in the preface that our dad wore the same ties for years, and there's no reason not to. Avoiding fashion doesn't mean you have to look frumpy. It simply means buying clothes that are tasteful and timeless—well-tailored suits or sport coats in classic colors for men, and traditional skirt suits for women. Invest in simple, solid-color dress shirts and conservative tie patterns that won't look silly next year. Take good care of clothes that require dry cleaning. If you buy a clothing brush and clean off your wool suit after each wearing, then hang it carefully, you can wear it many, many times before it needs professional cleaning. Those dry cleaning bills really add up—as you found out when you created a snapshot of your expenses.

Trend-proof casual clothes for men and women include khaki

Financial Foot Soldiers

David: Jonathan, you're the only guy I know who can talk knowledgeably about women's shoes. Great bar trick! But I don't get the shoe thing. Ladies' footwear seems to change with every season. The styles are so expensive, and they look like they're made of nothing. And they can't be comfortable. How many pairs of these things can a hardworking woman afford every year? I mean, I buy a pair of shoes—high-quality, comfortable shoes, I might add—and they last me *at least* five years, maybe ten if I'm careful with the shoe trees. When I replace them, I buy shoes of *the exact same style*-and no one notices the difference! Here's a true confession: I have worn the same shoes on the *Today* show for more than a year. I bet you have, too. Do you think a female coworker could get away with that? Women are getting ripped off in the shoe department, and it's hurting their bottom line.

Jonathan: David, I can't take you anywhere. As you well know, after college I worked as a buyer of women's shoes for Gimbels department store in New York, which explains why I know from Manolos. Most women *love* shoes, and you need to get over it. I would agree that nobody should overspend on clothing, especially on fashionable footwear that breaks the budget. But for many women with discretionary income cool shoes are a hobby. For them, shoes are like fishing gear, or truck accessories, or fine wine is to us guys. What's wrong with that? Indulgences are okay so long as you live within your budget—in fact, rewards like cool shoes or a new fly rod are a great way to inspire thriftiness, if they're pegged to savings in other areas. Most women I know would take a new pair of Blahniks over digital cable TV any day.

slacks, jeans, polo shirts, pullover sweaters—whatever makes you comfortable. Except in Hollywood and Palm Beach, really rich people almost *never* wear clothes like those in the ads in *GQ* and *Vogue*. (Apple founder Steve Jobs wears nothing but jeans and black shirts, which has perhaps become a fashion statement in itself.) Trying to look rich is a good way to stay poor.

The same goes for hairstyles. Choose looks that are low maintenance, so you don't have to go back to the barber or stylist every other week. That reminds us of an old joke: What's the difference between a good haircut and a bad haircut? A week and a half.

5. Stop paying sidewalk tax.

Sidewalk tax is what you pay every time you walk past an ATM and stick in your card for a quick cash infusion. ATMs are certainly convenient, but they can be budget wreckers, because most of that money you pull out just vanishes. Where does it all go? On little stuff you hardly think about, like snacks, coffee, magazines—impulse purchases you can avoid once you have a budget and start *thinking* about them. And if you use some other bank's machine, you're also paying fees that add up.

To get control over sidewalk tax, you need to do a little work: for three months, write down every single purchase you make with cash. Use a little notebook. You will probably be amazed at how much you spend on, well, nothing. Transfer the amounts into your budget snapshot. (By the way, the more stuff you buy with a debit card or a check, the less cash you'll need and the less stuff you'll have to write down in the notebook.) Most people can trim a lot of fat off their expense list just by cutting back on sidewalk tax.

After three months, you should have a pretty good handle on where your cash goes. At that point you can figure out cuts that help get your budget in line, then start paying yourself an "allowance" that covers only those necessary cash expenses. Once you have a weekly allowance and stick to it, you can stop keeping track of where each penny goes—unless you want to. Play a game with yourself. See how long you can go without refueling at the ATM. Take pride in *not* spending money unnecessarily!

6. Save on the small print (and don't be afraid to ask questions).

We've talked about unnecessary bank fees that can nibble away at your budget. Other folks are also trying to take a thousand little cuts from your hard-earned money. That "free" ticket you earned with your frequent-flyer miles? Guess again. Most now have service fees of $25 or more. In fact, the privilege of speaking to a human when you book an airline ticket over the phone will add $5 to the ticket price. You can avoid the fee, and maybe get a better deal, by booking on the airline's Web site.

Note that online travel agencies such as Expedia also charge a transaction fee of $5 or more. Some people find the best deal on Expedia, then go to the airline's Web site to book the ticket, saving themselves five bucks. Don't feel bad for Expedia; the company knows a savvy buyer can do that, but it also knows most people can't be bothered and will just pay the fee.

Paying attention to the details can really pay off. Marilyn, a sixty-one-year-old postal worker in Alaska, woke on New Year's Day 2004 with a severe pain in her stomach. She drove herself to the nearest hospital (her husband, Ron, was out of the state) where doctors performed an emergency appendectomy. Some minor complications required a follow-up procedure.

Eight months later, the bill arrived—for more than $45,000, almost a quarter of which wasn't covered by insurance. "I was absolutely floored," says Marilyn. "I never dreamed it would be that expensive." Ron and Marilyn requested an itemized bill and were shocked by the voluminous expense list, including $46 for two surgical gowns. They contacted Nora Johnson at Medical Billing Advocates of America (MBAA), who identified several extraneous charges and had them dropped from the bill.

What's more, the hospital hadn't informed Marilyn's insurer that her procedures were emergencies—an oversight that increased the couple's charges by $4,500. Under pressure from the couple and Johnson, the hospital forgave all but $500 of the bill. "I think most people would have just paid that bill without realizing it was excessive," says Marilyn. "People need to be aware that the hospital will bill them for every little thing—and they should make sure they're not being overcharged."

The health care system's complexity makes it ripe for abuse. Hospitals overcharge consumers and insurance companies $10 billion per year, according to an MBAA estimate—that's $1,300 *per hospital stay.* "I've examined thousands of hospital bills," says MBAA's Johnson. "All but two have included excessive charges." Her hospital-billing hall of shame includes a $1,000 charge for a toothbrush and a $129 fee for a "mucous collection system"—a box of tissues.

Johnson recommends that patients demand an itemized hospital bill (hospitals are required to provide one if you ask, but they may not otherwise). Don't be dismayed if the bill looks like it's written in a foreign language. Look closely and you might spot some obvious overcharges—for example, there shouldn't be a charge for penicillin if you're allergic to it.

What's more, hospitals' and insurance companies' billing procedures often cause consumers to pay unnecessary out-of-pocket charges. One reason: some of the doctors who attend to you during a hospital stay may not participate in your insurance plan's network—even if the hospital does. As a result, consumers often have to pay 30 percent or 40 percent co-payments on large portions of their hospital bills. Likewise, many insurance plans are supposed to pay a higher percentage of bills for emergency care—but sometimes they fail to do so. Such costs are one reason that medical bills contribute to half of all personal bankruptcies, according to a Harvard study.

Study your insurance plan to determine what it pays for and what it doesn't. And before you check in for a procedure, find local radiologists, anesthesiologists, and pathologists who are affiliated with your plan. Then write a letter to the hospital identifying those physicians, and explaining that you won't pay for out-of-network doctors. Make sure to keep a copy of the letter.

KNOCK DOWN
THE HOUSE OF CARDS

It's possible that after taking several passes through your expenses and finding the free money—cutting back on meals and entertainment, buying fewer clothes, vowing to keep the old car running longer, watching out for hidden and unnecessary fees—you're still spending more than you earn. If so, the problem is most likely an elephant in the room called debt.

Our generation, as a rule, is drowning in debt. So is our nation, which means we're passing our problems down to our children instead of solving them right now. Governments can get away with ignoring debt—at least for a while—because the creditors (bond holders) know that if things get really bad, politicians can always raise taxes or print more money. Don't you wish you had those options?

You don't. As a result, although your credit card doesn't say this, you should avoid buying things you cannot afford. Maybe credit cards should be required to have a warning, like cigarettes:

> **CAUTION: THE CHAIRMAN OF THE FEDERAL RESERVE BANK HAS DETERMINED THAT CREDIT CARD DEBT WILL DESTROY YOUR ABILITY TO SAVE FOR THE FUTURE, MAKE IT IMPOSSIBLE TO REACH LONG-TERM GOALS, AND LEAVE YOU POOR IN RETIREMENT**

The explosion of credit card use in our society is downright scary. In theory, credit cards cost you nothing, so long as you pay off the balance every month. But for most people, it doesn't work that way. Here's the truth:

- Three of five American families can't pay off their credit cards at the end of the month. Their running balance averages about $11,000, which is one-fourth of the average family's annual income.

- Current outstanding debt on U.S. credit cards—that's the "revolving" part that we don't pay off every month—totals nearly $800 billion, up from just $50 billion in 1980.

- Americans put $1.5 trillion worth of stuff on credit cards annually. Since most of it is stuff we can't pay for when the bill comes due, we will pay trillions more in interest over time.

- In the 1990s, credit card debt held by Americans living below the poverty level more than doubled.

- The average undergraduate owes even before entering the workplace, with almost $2,800 charged on plastic. That doesn't include student loans.

- Senior citizens, once noted for their frugality, are sinking deeper into debt; their average credit card balance increased by 89 percent between 1992 and 2001.

- If you only make the minimum payment on your credit card, it can take as long as thirty-one years to pay it off—assuming you stop charging more stuff.

These statistics would shock our grandparents, who could not imagine such irresponsible behavior—on the part of consumers *and* banks, the latter of which all too often encourage bad spending habits. It wasn't always that way. Back in the 1950s, banks introduced credit cards as a convenience for good customers who could be counted on to pay the bill every month. The business grew steadily but remained fairly genteel until the 1980s, when a series of state and federal deregulations made it possible for banks to charge more interest and operate nationally. Higher interest rates offset the risk of consumer default, encouraging banks to offer more credit to more people, and nationwide marketing opened the floodgates. In 2003, banks mailed out 5.2 billion offers for credit cards.

Today, more than 75 percent of American families use credit cards, which make it possible to rent cars, shop for deals on the Internet, buy plane tickets, and pay at the pump. But banks earn more interest when people stretch out their payments over longer periods; that's why minimum payments on credit cards shrunk at one point to as little as 1 percent of the total balance. With payments that small, it sounds so easy. But over the long term, you'll pay dearly in interest. Here's how to beat the banks.

1. Pay attention to the rate.

If you must carry a balance, one way to minimize your contribution to the card companies' coffers is to pay as much as you can on your highest-rate cards (while maintaining minimum payments on your other cards). Credit card companies will seize any excuse to raise your interest rate—so don't give them one. Late payments can trigger rates of as high as 30 percent or more, and also typically incur fees of between $30 and $40. What's more, some card companies recently have begun doubling or even tripling interest rates for cardholders who make late payments to other, completely unrelated creditors—so it's critical to stay on top of all your bills' due dates.

2. Pay on time.

Banks argue that late payments indicate credit risk, justifying higher rates. But in recent years banks seem to have redefined what's risky, often raising rates and charging penalties if a payment is late by a few minutes. According to www.cardweb.com, credit card late fees charged to consumers rose from $1.7 billion in 1996 to $7.3 billion in 2003.

3. Don't pay for "convenience."

Beware of "convenient" credit card features like cash advances, which come at substantially higher interest rates than do purchases. Likewise, card companies tend not to advertise the fact that they'll allow you to exceed your credit limit—and then charge you a recurring fee of about $40 per month as long as your balance remains above it.

Card firms will keep coming up with new ways to add to your debts, so it's vital to check your statement carefully every month and demand explanations for any charge that you don't understand.

Don't fall for quick-cash schemes.

Usurious lenders increasingly use aggressive marketing to target low-income Americans with promises of quick cash—as long as they lay down their car title, next paycheck, or tax refund as collateral.

The advertisements for such loans don't mention their costs, and for good reason: the effective interest rates are exorbitant, often running to annualized rates of 300 percent or more. "These loans can be extremely dangerous," says Jean Ann Fox, a spokesperson for the Consumer Federation of America. "For example, if you can't pay off your auto-title loan, you'll lose your car. That might prevent you from getting to work, making a bad situation even worse."

Likewise, rental firms persistently push rent-to-own arrangements as a convenient way for low-income consumers to own high-priced items they can't afford. These rental agreements are essentially high-rate loans, and they typically cost consumers more than double the price of the original item.

Beware of mortgage lenders that promise you the home of your dreams even if you have bad credit or a recent bankruptcy. Costly tricks include:

- Fees of as much as 5 percent of a loan's total value; legitimate mortgages charge 1 percent or less.
- Prepayment penalties that cost up to six months' interest if you pay ahead, for example by refinancing the loan.
- "Yield spread premiums," a fancy term for kickbacks to mortgage brokers.

4. Beware of credit counselors.

When you fall deeply into debt, you are especially vulnerable to financial predators. Many so-called credit-counseling agencies take advantage of debtors' desperation by charging outrageous fees—often equal to one month's debt payment plus recurring monthly charges. As if that's not bad enough, the agencies often don't disclose that they keep the initial fee rather than sending it to creditors. As a result, clients unwittingly miss payments, which takes their credit rating from bad to worse.

Some legitimate credit counselors do offer helpful programs to reduce interest rates, handle payments, and provide financial education. These agencies, most of which are affiliated with the National Foundation for Credit Counseling (NFCC), charge about $25 to begin a counseling program, followed by monthly fees of about $12. The NFCC's Web site (www.nfcc.org) can point you to an affiliated credit counselor in your area. Be aware, however, that even NFCC-affiliated agencies have been the subject of controversy, due to the fact that they receive much of their funding from the credit card industry.

Look for an agency that emphasizes consumer education. The counselor should spend at least a half-hour discussing your overall financial situation, not just your credit card debt, and should discuss a variety of options to address your credit problems—not just the agency's consolidation plan. Before signing up for a debt-payment program, make sure the counselor explains precisely what benefits it will provide, how much your monthly payments will be, and what percentage of those payments will go toward paying down your debt.

It's easy to get snared by card rates and fees. As a professional bookkeeper, thirty-three-year-old Elissa is pretty savvy about money. Still, when she was in her twenties she managed to rack up $22,000 in credit card debt. After missing some payments in the summer of 2005, she soon found herself paying an average annual interest rate of about 28 percent, meaning almost every penny of her $565 monthly payments was consumed by interest. "I was paying all I could afford, but my balances weren't going down," she says.

Elissa, who lives in upstate New York, exacerbated her plight when she unknowingly exceeded one card's credit ceiling. That mistake triggered a $40 monthly fee until she got her balance under its limit—a difficult proposition given the card's sky-high interest rate, which pushed the balance continuously higher, and her own cash-flow trouble.

Elissa briefly considered filing for bankruptcy, but ultimately signed up for a debt consolidation program offered by Consumer Credit Counseling. That program reduced her average interest rate to about 8 percent, helping her get on track to have her cards paid off in about four years. "I finally see the light at the end of the tunnel," says Elissa. "Reading the fine print would have saved me a lot of pain."

Check your credit report yourself.

Your credit rating has become critical to daily life. It's evaluated by potential employers, landlords, insurance companies, utilities, and government officials, in addition to loan officers; mistakes on your report can lead to higher interest payments and rejections for loans and other services. You are entitled to review a free copy of your credit report from the three nationwide credit agencies, Experian, TransUnion, and Equifax. Check every item listed on your credit reports. If you find inaccuracies, immediately report them in writing to the credit bureaus and the listed creditor.

Don't fall for certain companies' claims that they can fix a poor credit rating. If your reports are accurate, only two things can improve them: time and better credit habits (such as paying down debt or canceling credit cards). Firms that claim to repair credit typically charge hundreds of dollars just to review your credit reports, something you can do yourself for free.

Ultimately, the way to get out of the credit-card hole is to stop using credit cards. (See Tools for the Money, at the end of the chapter, for ways to pay down debt quickly.) A debit card linked to your checking account comes with virtually the same benefits as a "real" credit card, but you can only spend what you have. Once you climb out of debt, you can start a rainy-day fund (keep it in a money market account) to cover emergencies—perhaps three months' income. You can have savings deducted automatically from your now free-and-clear paycheck. Once you have *that*—and have learned to live within your means—your long-term goals will start coming into focus.

Some advisors say it's better to pay off your high-interest debts first, rather than in order of the payment-to-payoff ratio. That does make sense if you are not paying off all your debt at once. But the above technique will leverage the most money toward a total debt payoff, including the mortgage.

Debt guru Dave Ramsey suggests paying off debts in order of their actual size—meaning the payoff amount itself—starting with the smallest debt. His reasoning is psychological: paying off that first debt will inspire you to keep going. Maybe so, but that emotional boost will cost you more money down the road, since the high-interest loans will still be accumulating. If you need the boost of a quick win, go ahead and do it his way. Choosing *any* snowball method is better than doing nothing.

MANAGE YOUR MORTGAGE

People often talk about "good debt" and "bad debt." In truth, there is no good debt from a consumer's standpoint—in an ideal world we would all pay cash for everything—although some types of debt are easier to justify than others. Your home mortgage is

There's no place like home (equity).

During the last few years, rising home values and low interest rates led to a surge in home equity loans as people cashed in on their property. We saw folks doing the craziest things with these loans—buying fancy cars, taking vacations, paying off credit cards. Using your home as a bank is a bad idea. If housing prices drop, you could owe more on your home than it's worth. If you lost your job or got transferred and had to sell, you would have to come up with a way to pay back the bank, or be in default on your loan.

While a bank doesn't care what you do with the money you borrow against your home, we do. A home equity loan should only be used to make long-term improvements to the home itself. We mean improvements that will be sold to the next owner, not a 50-inch flat-screen TV. Studies have shown that the improvements most likely to increase a home's value include extra bedrooms, larger bathrooms, and renovated kitchens, within reason. Despite what you see in magazines, most people are not willing to pay thousands of dollars for six-burner dual-fuel stoves and other premium appliances. Unless your home is located in an extremely affluent neighborhood, you're not likely to make back that investment.

One of the worst "improvements" you can make is a swimming pool. For every potential buyer who wants a pool, another is actively opposed to owning one. (The exception might be a pool-crazy place like Southern California.) If you think you might sell your house in the next few years, do not add a pool.

often cited as good debt because homes *usually* increase in value, offsetting the cost of the loan. Borrowing for a home allows you to build equity while providing essential shelter.

Unfortunately, recent high home prices have ushered in a kaleidoscopic array of mortgage products that allow buyers to afford ever more expensive homes. That affordability is seriously compromised by huge financial risks. Consider one of the most insidious deals, the so-called option adjustable-rate mortgage, or option ARM. It sounds too good to be true (and don't we all know what that means): a mortgage with an annual rate of *as low as 1 percent!* The deal gets even better: the homeowner can actually *choose how much to pay*. Wow! Where do I sign?

Now, we should all know better than to believe this will work

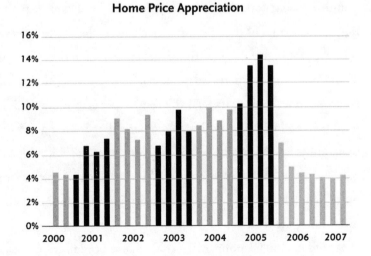

Home Price Appreciation

Source: National Association of Realtors, National Association of Realtors Forecast

out well. Didn't our parents teach us that there's no such thing as a free lunch? Yet, for a while in 2005, option ARMs accounted for more than *30 percent* of jumbo mortgages (defined that year as those exceeding $359,650), especially in California, where the cost of an average house far exceeds three times the average income, a traditional measure of the maximum you can afford in a home.

Most borrowers do realize that the incredibly low introductory rate of an option ARM is only good for a few months. After that, the interest rate jumps to a more normal 6 percent or 7 percent and can go up from there. But hey, if that's too rich for you, feel free to choose your own monthly payment (certain minimums apply). They don't call it an option ARM for nothing. But get a magnifying glass for the fine print: making nothing but the minimum payment (often less than the interest itself) can actually *increase* the value of the loan. In other words, the money you've "chosen" not to pay this month will get tacked on to the back end of the mortgage as increased principal—with more interest, of course. Some choice! It's called negative amortization, and it sounds like something you'd buy in a dark alley from a guy with brass knuckles. According to the *Wall Street Journal*, the unpaid balance on a $400,000 option ARM can actually increase to more than $450,000 after six years, assuming you make only the minimum payment.

As of late 2005, option ARMs have started to fall from grace, thanks to higher rates that make their "charms" less evident.

That's a good sign. If this is the only way you can afford a home, you need to be buying a cheaper home. Besides keeping the rain off your head, a house should be a positive investment in your future, not a potential land mine.

In most cases, the best way to finance a home is with a fixed-rate mortgage and a minimum 20 percent down payment. Most people get a thirty-year mortgage, but fifteen is often better. The difference in your monthly payment will only be a few hundred dollars because you'll be paying so much less interest. But the difference after fifteen years will be dramatic: the thirty-year loan is half paid off, while the fifteen-year loan is over. You're free and clear, and still young enough to enjoy it!

How much home can you afford? Probably not as much as you'd like. Your mortgage payment, combined with your property tax and home insurance, should total no more than 28 percent of your gross family income. What's more, total household debt should be no more than a third of your gross income. So if you and your spouse are making two car payments and shouldering massive student loans, your housing debt "comfort range" could be even less than 28 percent. Don't buy too much home! *If that means you can't afford any home in your area, you are better off renting until your financial situation improves.* Home ownership is a great thing, but not at any price.

The Debt Accelerator Payoff Method

This famous "snowball" technique has been shown in most cases to wipe out all debt in just a few years. That's a lot better than making minimum credit card payments for decades!

1. To begin, you need to find a way to apply 10 percent of your gross, or pretax, income to your debt. This is the accelerator, and finding it in your budget is the hardest part. But it *can* be done. Eliminate all extraneous purchases, like meals out, entertainment, and expensive groceries. Buy only clothes you absolutely need to stay warm and covered. If necessary, sell any car for which you owe more than a year's worth of payments and buy a cheaper car with cash. You can get a better car later, when you're debt-free. This is war!

2. Once you have your 10 percent accelerator accounted for, make a list of all your debts. You can even include your mortgage, which will make the payoff take longer but will leave you completely debt-free in an average of 7.5 years. Write down the total payoff (your outstanding balance) for each debt. You might have to call creditors to get the exact amount. Then divide the total payoff by the monthly payment. The resulting factor will be used to determine which debt to pay off first. For example, if you have $2,000 remaining on a car loan, and your monthly payment

is $200, your "factor" is 10. If you owe $1,000 on a credit card and your minimum payment is $50, your factor is 20.

3. Arrange your debts in order of the factor you have just created with your division exercise, starting with the smallest factor first. That debt, Number One, is the first to be paid off, since you can accomplish that in the fewest installments.

4. Make only the regular payments on all the other debts. For revolving credit, make the minimum payment. On Debt Number One, make the regular payment plus the entire 10 percent accelerator margin.

5. When Debt One is paid off, move on to Debt Two, this time making the regular payment, plus the accelerator margin, *plus* the regular payment you were making on Debt One. When Debt Two is paid off, tackle Debt Three, this time applying the accelerator margin, plus *both* regular payments on Debts One and Two. And so on.

Chapter Four:

Saving More Money Starting Now!

W e were back home visiting our parents over the holidays when the subject of finance came up. (It usually does when we're together!) We were discussing our nation's lousy savings rate, and why it isn't higher. Our dad grabbed a candy cane off the Christmas tree and held it up. "When you're in your twenties," he said, "you're saving for a home, paying off student loans, starting a family—and probably not saving a whole lot for retirement." He snapped off about a third of the candy cane. "In your thirties, you're making mortgage payments, raising kids . . . that eats up money you could be saving." He snapped off another section of the cane, leaving just the hook, and ran his finger along the part that curves back. "This is your retirement," he continued.

"You're actually going backward because you're spending and not earning." Off came the hook, leaving just a small straight section of the cane remaining in his hand. "This is your forties and fifties," he said, "when most people start seriously saving for retirement." He added, "It can be done. But, realistically speaking, you'll have to work really hard at it."

Nobody likes to save, although it's unclear why. We all *want* to save, we know it's necessary, but something else always seems to get in the way, right? If we can just pay off that car, *then* we'll start saving. Once that big raise comes through, *then* I'll start saving. After I pay off my credit card balance, I'll really ramp up my savings. . . .

But for too many of us that day never comes.

Part of the problem is the relentless tide of media that has been washing over us since we were kids. We are constantly being urged to buy more, upgrade, and add on. It started with the Hula-Hoops, pet rocks, and roller skates; then it was Levi's and Hush Puppies, followed by minivans and SUVs. Now it's plastic surgery and upscale retirement communities! The advertising is only part of it; on TV and in movies, music, and magazines, we're shown what the good life looks like—and how, if you spend enough money, you'll get there, too.

Exacerbating the problem is your neighbor:

"Joanne just bought the cutest new Gucci handbag!"

($375)

"Looks like Steve has a new Beemer."

($599 per month lease)

"Did you guys check out Pat's new titanium driver?"

($495)

"You haven't *lived* if you don't have a steam shower."

($22,000)

And so it goes, on and on, to the point where America has one of the lowest savings rates of any western nation. (In fact, our nation's savings rate is currently negative!)

You can't fix America's savings problem, but you can fix your own savings and set yourself up for a secure retirement. *The way to start is by starting.*

It's that simple. And the sooner you start, the better. That

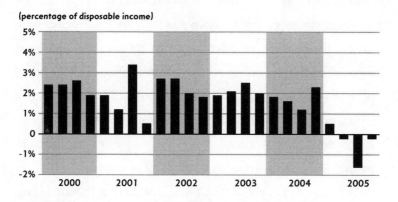

Personal Saving Rate

Source: U.S. Bureau of Economic Analysis

means accelerating payments on your high-interest obligations, such as credit cards (as we explainedin Chapter Three) to get out of debt as quickly as possible. Only then can you really start to build your wealth. If you can strive to save 10 percent to 15 percent of your gross income regularly, you'll soon reach the more rewarding aspects of financial planning—like what to do with those growing savings! That's where it gets fun. In this chapter, we'll explain how to:

- Start the saving habit right now, even if you're getting older.
- Save painlessly and automatically.
- Avoid or defer taxes on your savings (legally).

We've all heard the phrase "time is money." Usually it's a negative connotation that comes to mind when a plumber is standing in the kitchen with a wrench in his hand. But that phrase takes on a *positive* meaning when it comes to saving money. The reason is simple: time is a key ingredient in the recipe of compounded savings. An average rate of return on your money over a short period of time will give you an unspectacular result. That same average return over a long period can yield millions. Really! Time is what makes your money work for you; the whole concept of compounding interest is set up to benefit you over time.

How exactly does it work? Consider twin brothers named, say, David and Jonathan. Both are twenty-five years old. Or at least they were at one time. David invests $4,000 annually in an IRA for eight years, then stops.

Meanwhile Jonathan, carefree lover of life, spends those eight years traveling the world, getting in touch with his inner twin, not saving anything, but having a blast. He comes home, settles down, and starts saving $4,000 a year in a Roth IRA, just when David quits saving. Jonathan decides he likes saving. He keeps right on saving, for years and years—*thirty-two* years, in fact, right up to his retirement at age sixty-five. David, meanwhile, *hasn't saved one dime* since he turned thirty-three.

To recap: David saves eight years, then lives like there's no tomorrow for thirty-two years. Jonathan lives like there's no tomorrow for eight years, then saves for thirty-two years. So who has more money at age sixty-five? (Hint from David: They say firstborns are more intelligent, even if the age spread is only four minutes.)

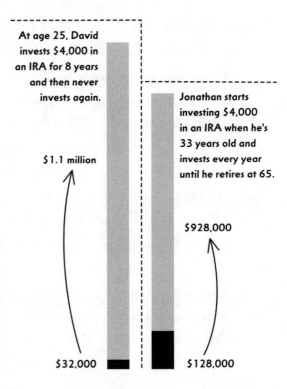

At age 25, David invests $4,000 in an IRA for 8 years and then never invests again.

Jonathan starts investing $4,000 in an IRA when he's 33 years old and invests every year until he retires at 65.

$1.1 million

$928,000

$32,000

$128,000

You knew the answer, right? It's David, the early starter. He retires with $1.1 million, while Jonathan has $928,000. (These numbers assume an average annual stock market performance of 10 percent.) And don't forget: David invested a grand total of $32,000, while Jonathan had to stash away $128,000. Because he started late, Jonathan has to save *four times as much* as David, and still retires with less. The moral of the story: start early!

Actually, there's another moral to this story. You'll notice that both David and Jonathan retire with significant savings, from saving *a measly $333 a month*. That's $76.92 a week, or about the cost of dinner for three at a Thai restaurant. (Which would you prefer: green curry shrimp or retiring a millionaire?) So the second moral is, it's better to start late than not to start at all. By the way, you can find savings calculators all over the Web (check out www.choosetosave.org) and plug in your own numbers.

Obviously, starting early is so much easier, because the real miracle of compounding occurs toward the end of the savings period. That's when you're compounding money upon money that's been compounding for years.

Pre-tax, payroll-deducted savings like a 401(k) are the easiest, fastest way for the average person to build wealth.

In fact, all of the various tax-deferred programs were designed by the federal government precisely to encourage normal folks like you and me (well, us) to save more money. The government loses gazillions in potential tax revenue on these plans, but the tradeoff is deemed to be worth it because future savings are in the

How to describe compounding

Jonathan: When I go to schools to teach kids about money, I always ask them, "What would you rather have, $1 million in your hands, or one penny doubled every day for a month?" The kids usually opt for the cool million—until I explain that a penny doubled every day for thirty days would add up to more than ten million dollars! The reason, of course, is that by day twenty-nine you're only halfway there, dollarwise.

David: Pretty good. But I prefer the story of the wise slave who saves the life of his king. The ruler offers him any gift in return, so the slave replies that his needs are simple: all he wants is a grain of rice on the first square of a chess table, with double the number of grains on each succeeding square. The king laughs at this simpleton's request—he could have asked for diamonds and gold—until his bursar figures out that by the sixty-fourth square he would need more rice than had been grown since the beginning of time. The slave became the wealthiest man in the kingdom.

You need to get into that chess game now! And the easiest way to start is at that place you go every day—your job. You undoubtedly know that there are ways to have retirement savings automatically deducted from your paycheck *before* taxes, thereby reducing your taxable income. Chances are good you're one of the more than 42 million Americans who contribute to 401(k)-type retirement plans at work. But do you put in the maximum? If not, you are selling yourself short.

interest of our nation. If Uncle Sam is *that* willing to cut you some slack on taxes, you should pay attention. Here are the options:

LET YOUR WORK
WORK FOR YOU

David: A 401(k) retirement plan, in my opinion, is the single most important investment vehicle of your life. We can't depend on the government to provide a secure retirement. We've seen that we can't depend on corporate pensions, either. This is the easiest and smartest way to save for the future, with the greatest reward.

Jonathan: Good point, but what about your house? Lots of people consider their house to be their biggest investment. In fact, many Americans assume they can sell the big house at retirement, then live off the gain.

David: Well, as someone who has moved around a lot, I can tell you that homes can *sometimes* reap windfall profits. Trouble is, a home isn't very liquid; even in a hot market, it takes time to make and close a deal—waiting for inspections and appraisals, you name it. And unlike paper assets, your home has practical value—it keeps the rain off your head—so selling it means buying or renting something else. If your home has gained a lot in value, it's likely your next home will also cost more. So unless you are really scaling back or moving to a much cheaper community, the money

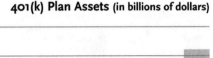

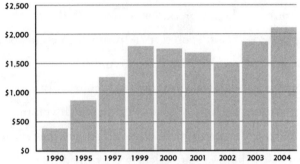

Source: Investment Company Institute, U. S. Department of Labor, and Federal Reserve Board

you gain on the sale is likely to get rolled into your next home. Meanwhile, moving itself is expensive and stressful.

Jonathan: I agree, even if I haven't moved as often as you! And what worries me is that lots of people use the home-as-an-investment line to justify a lot of luxury renovations they can't really afford. You're better off investing in a 401(k), *along* with building home equity.

The basics of 401(k) plans—and the similar 403(b)s, which cover nonprofit organizations—are established by federal law, but the details vary from company to company. In essence, you tell your company to deduct a portion of your pretax income automatically from your paycheck (in 2006, up to $15,000 annually for workers under age fifty, but individual companies could specify lesser amounts). The money gets invested in a variety of accounts that you choose. (Some companies offer more choices than others.)

In return for the tax break, you can't touch the money (with certain exceptions) until you turn $59^{1}/_{2}$, at which point you must pay income tax on any withdrawals. And you *must* start withdrawing money (known as minimum required distributions or MRDs) starting on April 1 of the year in which you turn $70^{1}/_{2}$. That's because the government wants to get its taxes eventually. The annual withdrawals are calculated by dividing the value of your account by the number of years you can be expected to live, according to the Uniform Distribution Table. You can find the table all over the Web; one good site is www.rcre.rutgers.edu/money/ira-table.asp. One exception: if you are still working for the same company at age $70^{1}/_{2}$, and you own less than 5 percent of the company, you don't have to start minimum withdrawals until the year after you retire.

Here's the really cool part: many companies will actually *match* your contributions, up to a certain amount. (Sometimes the match is in company stock.)

Let's say you work for a company that pays you $50,000 a year, and you put 6 percent, or $3,000, annually into your 401(k). Now let's say your company matches half that contribution, depositing a free $1,500 into your 401(k) account every year. After twenty years, assuming the stock market average return, that matching contribution alone—not including your own money—will have earned nearly $100,000. Over thirty years, it will earn nearly $300,000. Over a forty-year career, you will have earned *just under $800,000!*

And that doesn't count all the money of your own that you've been socking away. Nor does it take into account annual pay raises, which presumably will increase your contributions as well as the company match.

By the way, companies don't give you free money out of the goodness of their hearts. They do it to encourage enrollment; in order to meet federal guidelines, a certain percentage of employees must participate in the plan.

If you don't already contribute the maximum allowed in your company's 401(k), here's what you're missing:

- Enforced, automatic regular savings that you probably won't even miss in your budget.

- Tax-deferred growth for years and years, plus a reduction in your current income tax.

- Free matching money from your employer, in many cases.

This is truly an offer you can't refuse! Even so, there are potential pitfalls with employee savings plans. Here's what to watch out for:

1. Choosing the wrong investments.

Choice can be empowering—but sometimes it can be daunting. Faced with an array of confusing investment options in their 401(k) plans, many employees throw up their hands and make the worst possible choices. They put all their money into company stock (way too risky), or into a money market fund (way too safe). (We'll discuss better options in Chapter Six.)

2. Withdrawing early.

The whole idea here is saving for the future, so the government makes it painful to take money out before you turn $59^1/_2$. Besides paying federal, state, and local income tax on every penny you withdraw early, you'll also face a 10 percent penalty. There are some exceptions—like if you are fifty-five and you leave your job, or you are under court order to pay child support or alimony, if you become disabled, or you have medical bills exceeding 7.5 percent of your adjusted gross income.

Another way around the penalty is by withdrawing cash in what are called substantially equal periodic payments (SEPP, also known as IRS code 72[t]) for at least five years prior to turning $59^1/_2$. One situation in which a 72[t] distribution could make sense is if you have been disabled. When figuring out the distribution, you would ideally only withdraw returns on your investment, not the actual principal. And you would still have to pay taxes, just no penalty. 72[t]s can be complicated to figure out—taking into account your life expectancy and other factors—because you can't change your withdrawal amount later, and you must withdraw the entire amount. Hire a financial advisor if you think a SEPP account is right for you.

3. Losing your vesting.

If your company matches some or all of your 401(k) contributions, the matching portion is likely to be vested over a period of time—perhaps several years. Vesting simply means that the free money they've been giving you isn't really yours to keep until you've worked there for a while. The idea is to prevent employees from quitting after a year or so and taking a lot of company cash with them. To get your matching funds, you have to demonstrate loyalty. The vesting could be gradual, or all at once. (Vesting only applies to free company matches; your own contributions are always yours to keep.) Some people don't think about vesting when making a career change, and forfeit all that free money. Of course, if the dream job of your life comes along, take it! But if you have the ability to wait until you're vested, why not?

4. Not saving more at age fifty.

When you turn fifty, you are allowed to contribute more to a 401(k) plan—in 2006, as much as $5,000 more, depending on your company's rules. Make sure to boost your contribution to the maximum on that very important birthday. Remember the candy cane?

5. Not rolling over.

It's amazing how many times we see people change jobs, then take out their 401(k) money and cough up the taxes and the 10 percent penalty. It's as if the end of the job meant the end of their retirement savings. Bad idea! The smart thing to do is roll the money over into a 401(k) at your new job, or into an IRA (see below). Rollovers are easy, and you pay no penalties or taxes.

THE AMAZING IRA

Individual retirement accounts (IRAs) work a lot like 401(k) plans, except for individuals rather than for whole companies. You don't have to be self-employed to fund one; in fact you can have an IRA *and* a 401(k), although you may not be able to claim all of the IRA tax deductions, depending on your income and how much you contribute to your 401(k). In 2006, any working person (and the spouse of a working person) can contribute up to $4,000 ($5,000 if you're over fifty) to an IRA. So a married couple under fifty can sock away a total of $8,000 annually. Assuming you meet the guidelines, including (again, in 2006) modified adjusted gross income of under $75,000 for a married couple, that full amount is deducted from your taxable earnings. The money then grows tax-deferred until you take it out at retirement. As with a 401(k), you pay taxes when you withdraw money, and required minimum distributions begin the year you turn $70^{1}/_{2}$.

IRAs, however, are much more lenient about early withdrawals, allowing penalty-free (but not tax-free) distributions before age $59^{1}/_{2}$ for first-time home buyers (up to $10,000), college expenses, even health insurance if you lose your job and are receiving unemployment checks for at least twelve consecutive weeks. Still, IRAs are fairly stingy compared to 401(k)s. A married couple under fifty with two 401(k)s could stash up to $30,000 a year, tax-deferred—not including any employer matches. The same couple could contribute at best $8,000 to an IRA. One other potentially significant difference: 401(k)s are protected from creditors; IRAs are not.

Clearly, traditional IRAs play second banana to a good 401(k) plan. But there is another option: in 1996, Congress came up with the Roth IRA. Read on.

BOOMING ROTHS

Roth IRAs function in much the same way as traditional IRAs—including the same maximum contribution—but with one major difference: you get no tax deduction. What kind of a deal is that? Here's the second part of the difference: the money grows tax-free. Not tax-deferred, but *tax-free*. Forever.

Think about it. If you and your spouse deposit $8,000 annually ($666 per month) in a Roth IRA for thirty years, you may earn more than *$1.4 million* (based on the average annual S&P 500 return of 10 percent), and you will never pay a dime of taxes on it. When you die, your heirs will receive what's left over free of income tax, although estate taxes, if any, would apply.

Another nice feature of the Roth IRA is that there is no penalty for withdrawing your original contribution at any time. (You can't withdraw the tax-free investment growth you are earning before age $59^1/_2$, however, without facing taxes and penalties.)

Freeing you from the burden of future taxes is a great concept—in part because nobody knows what the tax code will look like in the future. Roth IRAs mean one less unpredictable factor in your retirement. Because of that, we think that, over the long term, Roth IRAs (named for their champion, the late Senator William V. Roth of Delaware) are a much better deal than traditional IRAs. In fact, you should consider converting your traditional IRAs into Roth IRAs, unless you are currently in a very high tax bracket. You will have to pay taxes (but no penalties) when you convert your traditional IRA, so you need to factor in that expense. But you will thank yourself later.

Roth IRAs have become so popular that Congress recently created a new retirement savings plan, one that promises to completely change the financial landscape: the Roth 401(k).

BLOOMING ROTHS

It had to happen. Now you can get all the tax-free growth of a Roth IRA in your 401(k) or 403(b)—but with substantially larger contributions. Starting in 2006, Americans who work for companies that choose to sponsor one of the new Roth 401(k) plans will be able to contribute up to $15,000 annually ($20,000 for those age fifty or over). It means sacrificing the tax break on the front end, but, as we saw with the Roth IRA, your long-term gain is incomparable. It could be argued that high-income earners will take a big hit on their current taxes—but, let's face it, taxes have rarely been lower. The highest individual income tax rate in 2006 drops to just 35 percent! Pay that relatively low tax now in return for huge tax savings later.

We encourage you to look at Roth 401(k)s if you have the choice. Alas, that's the key question. The government has authorized the new plan, but no company is required to offer it. If your company has not yet signed on, speak up, and let the head honchos know how important it is you.

THE SMALL
BUSINESS ADVANTAGE

These are all tax-deferred retirement plans designed to give small businesses and self-employed people the advantages of a pension or 401(k). The rules differ, but all require that the plans be available to certain employees of your business—not just the owner. (If you don't have any employees, it's all the easier.) The Simplified Employee Pension (SEP) plan requires a business owner to fund employees' IRA contributions—sort of like a mini-pension. A Savings Incentive Match Plan for Employees (SIMPLE) involves employee contributions to an IRA that are matched by the employer. As the name suggests, they are simple to set up, with virtually no paperwork. Keogh plans (there are several) are more complicated and harder to administer, but allow higher contributions than the other plans. If you're self-employed or run a small business, one of these programs is probably right for you. Consult your tax accountant to be sure you're making the right move.

Now that we've laid out the landscape of tax-deferred and tax-free savings plans, we get to tell you that it could all change in the near future. With fewer Americans covered by traditional pension plans, political leaders of both parties are eyeing ways to streamline retirement saving.

And some changes could be dramatic—such as eliminating the

entire spectrum of existing plans in favor of a one-size-fits-all system. Other proposals would involve smaller tweaks. Our best advice right now is to pay attention when your company announces changes in your benefit plan. Your tax advisor is also a good source of information. Until Congress makes up its mind, let's just keep saving—and move on to the next phase: what to do with the money!

Chapter Five

How to Get Rich the Prudent Way

You didn't think this was one of those get-rich-quick books, did you? As financial advisors, we make our living convincing people that you make money over time, not overnight. All too often, we see boomers do everything right—live within their means, avoid credit card debt, save for college and retirement—then implode by making rash investment decisions.

Could any of these people be you?

- Diane saw the stock market tumble for two years in 2001 and 2002. Finally, she couldn't take it anymore. She sold everything in a panic . . . right before the market rebounded in 2003.

• Chuck was sick from seeing the headlines in 1999. So many people making obscene amounts of money in technology stocks! And his account seemed to be standing still at the time. A neighbor told him about a popular dot-com stock fund and, although he didn't have a clue about the underlying holdings, Chuck plowed his entire retirement account into it. Six years later, his account is now (finally) back up to *half* of what it once was.

• Robin loses sleep because of the daily ups and downs of the stock market. Why didn't her broker sell before the market went down last week? Why didn't he buy that other fund that went up so much this year?

• Darin's portfolio has been a flatliner for five years. His account value was $87,658 on December 31, 2001. The December 2005 statement just arrived. Account value: $88,745. He says, "I should've just put it in a money market account." At his wit's end, he has lost hope in the stock market, and is now exploring a local real estate rental opportunity.

If you find yourself relating to Diane, Chuck, Robin, or Darin, don't feel bad: you are not alone! These are the stories we hear from investors nearly every day. Do you see the common theme? Words and phrases like "panic," "frustrated," "sick," "loses sleep," and "should have" are the signposts. Virtually all of these folks have turned investing into a full-time worry.

It doesn't have to be that way. Once you're saving money, you've already *done* the hard work. What follows should be easy! And it is, as long as you understand that it's not going to be a smooth ride. Yes, you can bet that if you invest in stocks or stock mutual funds, there will be periods of time when you lose money—serious money—sometimes for years at a time. But history also shows us that it's well worth it. You can avoid financial heartburn by following our seven favorite rules:

1. **Let time be your ally.** Focus on at least five to ten years out, and grow your wealth steadily through compounding.

2. **Maintain realistic expectations.** From 1928 to 2005, the S&P 500 has gained an average of about 10 percent annually, and experts often use that figure to calculate long-term returns. For your planning purposes, be more conservative. Use 8 percent to be safe.

3. **Diversify across asset classes.** Smart investors hold a mix of stocks, bonds, and commodities. The mix may vary depending on your age and temperament, but the basic principle of diversification holds true today.

4. **Hire a professional financial advisor you trust.** Let *him or her* worry about the market.

5. **Keep your costs down.** Look for investments with low fees, and don't do a lot of trading, which can generate higher commissions and taxes.

6. **Invest regularly.** Take advantage of dollar cost averaging to maximize returns.

7. **Don't worry too much about the market.**

If you follow these rules, you will win. They are time-tested and battle-proven over nearly 100 years of financial history. And don't worry, we'll explain everything. First, let's run down the various investment options, from stocks to bonds, real estate and commodities. Because even though you're better off not stressing out about your investments, a little bit of basic knowledge can't hurt.

THE BASICS OF INVESTING

There are two basic types of investments: equity and debt. Equity is when you own something—usually common stock in a company, but also real estate and commodities like gold. Debt, such as a bond, is when you loan money and receive interest in return.

As a general rule, equity is risky because stocks rise and fall, sometimes precipitously. Debt is safer because in order to lose your principal (that's the amount you invested in the first place), the government or company that owes you would have to actually default on the loan. It happens, but not often. One source cited a default rate of less than .05 percent over a thirty-year period.

As we have seen, the risk you take with equity is rewarded with a better return in the long term. *You need to take reasonable risk in order to grow your wealth.* Here's the math: let's say you save *20 percent* of your take-home pay over forty years in a "safe" account (like Treasury notes) with 4 percent annual growth. After deducting 3.5 percent inflation, at the end of forty years you'll have less than ten years of retirement income. That's not good enough! On the other hand, put that money into the stock market and assume 6 percent annual growth after inflation, and the money will last into decades of retirement. For most of your life, equity is where you want your money.

Investing in Equity

When you buy stock, you get a piece of the rock, so to speak. You're becoming a part owner in the company that issued the stock, and you're entitled to vote for officers, among other privileges. In most cases, you'll have very little actual control over the company; you are mainly buying the potential for growth. Many stocks also pay quarterly dividends, which we'll talk about soon.

The "stock market" is actually dozens of markets and exchanges all over the world. In the United States, the three most widely known markets are the New York Stock Exchange, the American Stock Exchange (what you see behind us during our New York segments on CNBC), and the NASDAQ, which is short for the National Association of Securities Dealers, Automated Quotation. When you tell a broker to buy 100 shares of IBM, he transmits your order to a salesman on the floor of the New York Stock Exchange. The salesman then finds someone willing to sell IBM shares. And the price? Well, the price is whatever buyer and seller agree is reasonable—which changes constantly. The stock market lives and dies by the rule of supply and demand.

Because so many people are buying and selling stock every day, for all sorts of reasons, it's virtually impossible to predict what will happen. In fact, professional money managers do not really attempt to "outsmart" the market. Instead, they look at historic trends and try to apply them to the current situation, while taking into account various factors that gauge a company's performance. Even if you never buy individual stocks, it's a good idea to understand how stock performance is measured. If nothing else, you might own some of your own company's stock (but, we hope, not too much, as former Enron employees can attest) and should be able to tell how it's doing. What follows is our stock primer:

1. Revenues

Revenues are what a company brings in for whatever it sells—not to be confused with earnings, which are what's left over after paying taxes and bills. Revenues won't tell you precisely how well a company is doing (it could be spending way too much to generate those revenues), but it's a good sign if revenues are growing from year to year. Such a company, under good management, is likely to thrive. In the nineties it became trendy to ignore revenues and earnings; all those sexy Internet startups would make money someday, right? Since the dot-com bubble burst, revenues have (sensibly) come back into fashion.

2. P/E ratio

The price/earnings ratio quantifies the price of a stock relative to its earnings. So if a company's stock costs $100 per share, and has earnings of $4 per share, you would divide 100 by four to get a P/E ratio of twenty-five. Historically, the stock market's P/E ratio has been about fourteen. A lower P/E ratio (such as ten or twelve) represents good value, and presumes less risk, because chances are that the company's stock price will increase dramatically in good times. Many investors looking for bargains focus on P/E ratios. But it's important to look at long-term earnings—say, the last five years—and not just the latest quarter.

A related indicator is P/E to growth, or PEG. This compares a company's P/E ratio to its annual earnings growth. Ideally, earnings growth should be the same as or higher than the P/E ratio—so if a company with a P/E of twenty-five has annual earnings growth of 25 percent, that would represent very good value.

3. Book value

Book value is the sum total of a company's actual assets, including cash, equipment, real estate, and so on, minus liabilities such as debt. It is almost always less than the total value of shares outstanding, but investors shopping for value often look for a low price-to-book ratio, meaning the price of a share is small compared to the total book value. Or, put another way, each share "buys" a larger chunk of actual equity. Companies with lots of equipment and infrastructure—like airlines or auto manufacturers—tend to have high book value, so your shares are buying more stuff. By contrast, Internet companies and other service businesses have low book values because they don't need a lot of equipment and factories to do business. As our economy becomes more service-oriented, the price-to-book ratio has become less meaningful.

4. Debt-to-equity ratio

Most companies take on debt to grow their business, although some take on more than others. (European companies typically carry less debt than American concerns.) If a company takes on too much debt, interest payments can eat into profits. So it's important to look at total debt relative to the value of outstanding shares—the debt-to-equity ratio. Ideally, this number should be a fraction less than one. If a company has more debt than equity, it could spell trouble in a business downturn.

5. Volume

Volume means the number of shares in a company that are trading at any moment. Investors pay attention to volume because it signifies interest in the stock—both good and bad. If the price drops on heavy volume, it means less demand for the stock. If, on the other hand, the price rises on heavy volume, that means greater demand is fueling the increase. Sometimes a stock price rises on low volume, which can mean the reasons behind the increase are unjustified.

6. Volatility

While no one can predict how a stock will perform in the future, some stocks have a history of swinging up and down more widely than others. Such volatility is expressed in a number using standard deviation known as a *beta*. A stock that tends to move at the same rate as the overall market has a beta of one. A beta of 1.3 means the stock has historically moved 30 percent more (both up and down) than the overall market. Similarly, a beta less than one indicates a stock is less volatile than the overall market. Knowing a stock's volatility can be helpful in deciding how much risk you want to take at any given time.

7. Dividends and yield

Dividends are profits that are paid back (usually quarterly) to shareholders. Not every company pays dividends; in some cases, companies choose instead to reinvest profits back into the company, or use them to pay CEOs outrageous bonuses. (Just kidding!) In the nineties, dividends fell from grace—in part because many high-flying Internet stocks simply had no dividends to pay out. (Economics 101: to pay dividends, you need to be making money.)

We're happy to report that dividends are back. In 2005 alone, there were more than 1,900 dividend increases! This is good news. We like dividends for a lot of reasons:

Jonathan: **Dividends really add up.** From 1926 to 2004, more than 40 percent of the S&P 500's annual rate of return has come from reinvested dividends.

David: **Dividends tame volatility.** Stocks that go up and down are stabilized by dividends, which provide a steady return, even in crazy times. During the bear market decline from March 2000 to September 2002, dividend-paying stocks had a weighted total return of –17.4 percent, while non-dividend-paying stocks fell 66.0 percent!

Jonathan: **Dividends indicate financial strength.** Since companies have the right to stop paying dividends when times are tough, those that pay and raise dividends are by definition sanguine about their current and future business environment.

David: **Dividends impose fiscal discipline on management.**
Companies with a long-standing dividend policy have an obligation to meet those quarterly payments.

How can you tell if a stock is paying a dividend? By its *yield,*
which expresses the percentage of a stock's price that is paid out
in annual dividends. So if you buy stock at $100 a share and it
pays out $3.50 per share in annual dividends, the yield is 3.5 per-
cent. The yield is constantly changing because the stock's price is
changing. But the dividend remains $3.50 per share—unless the
company changes how much it pays out in dividends. By the

Dividend-paying and non-dividend-paying stock performance

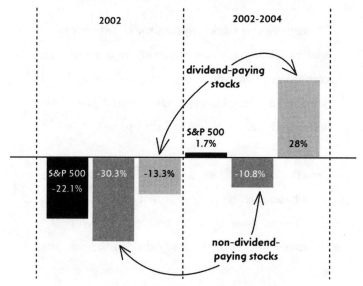

From: Federated Investors Inc.; Source: Standard and Poor's

way, dividends are taxable, although at only 15 percent for most taxpayers (for dividends from American and many foreign companies) since the tax cuts of 2003. In the meantime, you can always earn dividends completely tax-free in a Roth IRA or one of the new Roth 401(k)s.

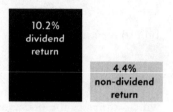

Total return on stocks from 1972-2004

10.2% dividend return

4.4% non-dividend return

From: Federated Investors Inc.;
Source: Standard and Poor's

Stocks that pay dividends are sometimes called income stocks. You might often hear that term, as well as a few others commonly used to describe the various types of stock:

- Although **income stocks** pay dividends, the term can be a bit misleading. Even these typically large, established companies can decide to pay less in dividends. So the "income" part is not totally predictable as it generally is with bonds (see "Investing in Debt," p. 105).

- **Growth stocks** rarely pay dividends. These companies are all about reinvesting in their business, which is expected to grow by leaps and bounds. What the shareholder loses in a steady dividend check, she gains (with luck) in share price. Technology companies are often growth stocks.

- **Value stocks** often pay dividends and trade at a discount to their future value. For whatever reason, the company's share price has dropped, becoming attractive to value investors.

- **Small-cap, mid-cap, and large-cap** are terms used to describe a company's size, as measured by is total market capitalization—the number of shares outstanding times the price per share. In general, small-cap companies have less than $1 billion in capitalization; mid-cap signifies $1 billion to $12 billion; and large-cap is more than $12 billion. (The mightiest large-cap stocks are called *blue chips*, which refers to the color of the most expensive poker chip on a gaming table.) These size distinctions can be important because small-cap stocks historically have provided greater returns, but with greater volatility and risk.

Commodities

Investors today often assume their asset classes are limited to stocks and bonds. They forget about commodities, also known as hard assets—everything from gold to lumber to natural gas to pork bellies. Commodities are traded in special exchanges around the world; two of the better known are the New York Mercantile Exchange (crude oil and precious metals) and the Kansas City Board of Trade (grain). We like commodities because, going way back to the 1800s, they've experienced cycles (lasting an average of eighteen years) that are not correlated to paper assets like stocks. That means when stocks are down, chances are good that commodities will be up. This is particularly true in periods of rising inflation. Understanding commodities is the work of specialists, however. So we usually recommend average folks invest in them through specialized mutual funds called sector funds. More on these later, under "The Feeling Is Mutual."

Commodities fell out of favor for more than a decade, but in the last couple of years, during the stagnant U.S. stock market, they bounced back. One downside to commodities is that they are less liquid than paper because the markets are thinner—so, in a down cycle, it could be harder to get out of them. Some commodities, like gold, do very well during times of geopolitical uncertainty.

Some of the most rabid callers on our radio show are "gold bugs" who are saying "I told you so!" Indeed, gold prices have been flying lately. But, frankly, as a long-term investment gold has never proved its mettle, pardon the pun. It's extremely cyclical, with lots of ups and downs. So gold investors have done very well over the past five years or so, but who knows what's next?

Check out these numbers: If you invested $100 in stocks and $100 in a precious metals index thirty years ago, you'd have a return of $3,603 from stocks and just $1,031 from the precious metals investment. Plus, stocks can pay income in the form of dividends. Having a little gold in your portfolio is okay. But you want to date gold, not marry it.

Real Estate

Investing in real estate can be another good cushion against the volatility of the stock market, and historically it has served as an inflation hedge. Also, owning property comes with many tax benefits—including the fact that you can *depreciate* buildings every year, even while their actual value is *appreciating*. But unlike passively investing in the stock market, managing properties is hard work—in fact, it's really an occupation. An easier way to diversify into real estate is by buying into real estate investment trusts, or REITs. These are traded like stocks and are very liquid, so you can easily sell. You can also invest in mutual funds that specialize in REITs.

Investing in Debt

Debt-based investments, including bonds, are basically IOUs. Only this time, they owe *you* money! Isn't that better than getting credit card bills in the mail? Ultimately, we're all investing for one reason: income. So if you're at a stage in your life when you need

Home is where the heart lies.

David: When Janet and I moved to the Seattle area in 1990, we bought a townhouse in Kirkland, right on Lake Washington, for $190,000. My parents thought we were lunatics to pay that much for a townhouse. Eleven months later, we sold it for $297,000. And most of that profit was "leveraged" because we earned it on borrowed money—our mortgage. We did the same thing several times again as we moved around the country. If your timing is good, there are few ways to grow your wealth faster than by buying and selling real estate.

Jonathan: As I watched David move from one house to another and make significant gains each time, I wondered, "Am I missing something here?" I've lived in the same house for years, and I always thought of it as a place to raise my family, not an investment. I'm sure I've missed some opportunities to cash in, but when the housing market goes sour (as it will someday!), I'll have no worries. They say real estate is all about location, location, location, but there's a fourth consideration: timing. Get it wrong, and you not only lose money but could find yourself without a place to live. I'll sit tight and enjoy my home sweet home, thank you very much.

investment income, it doesn't get any better than bonds, which mean regular checks in the mail.

What happens is, you loan money to a big entity like a government or a corporation, and you get paid back with interest. Loaning money to a government or a corporation is generally low risk, although it depends on which government or corporation, as we'll see. In return for that relative safety, over the long run you will probably make less money than you would by investing in equity. But, in the right situation, debt has many advantages.

For starters, the interest payments—in the form of monthly, semi-annual, or annual checks—provide regular, predictable income. This is a good thing when you are older and the short-term volatility of the stock market no longer makes sense. Plus, at the end of the debt term, which could be anywhere from a few days to many years, you are reasonably guaranteed to get back your principal. It's pretty simple in theory, but in practice there's more to it than that.

When you buy a bond, your interest rate is usually fixed. (There are exceptions, which we'll explain later.) That could be good, or it could be bad. Say you buy a $10,000, ten-year security at 6 percent interest. Every year, the government or company to which you loaned that money pays you $600 in interest. Now let's say that next year interest rates go down, and the latest version of that security is only paying 5 percent. Lucky for you, your rate is fixed at 6 percent, which puts you ahead of the pack. The current market value of your bond might increase to $11,000. In an economy where interest rates are falling sharply, bonds can be a great investment.

But suppose instead that interest rates are going up. Now the same bond can be purchased at 7 percent interest. Oops! Don't you feel like a dope? If you only had one of those shiny new bonds, you could be earning $700 in interest. (In the real world, you might not sweat the hundred bucks, but if you've got $1 million in retirement funds tied up in bonds, that's a hefty $10,000 annual difference. And if you need to live off that income, these interest swings can make you crazy.)

You may be interested to know that there's also a market for "used" bonds. Somebody would be willing to buy that $10,000 bond from you at a discount—say, $8,000. Why would anyone want a used bond? Because at that discount price, the buyer is effectively getting an interest rate of 7.5 percent, since he's still getting the guaranteed $600 annual interest, but on an $8,000 investment. And when the bond matures at the end of the ten-year loan period, he'll make a $2,000 profit when the government or corporation pays back the full $10,000 principal. Not a bad day at the office!

You can see from our examples that there is a direct relationship between bond prices and interest rates. When interest rates go down, bonds become more valuable, and their price rises. But when interest rates rise, bonds *lose* value, and their price drops. This seesaw is as close as anything comes in the world of finance to a sure thing, which is one reason why bonds are more predictable types of investments.

But they are not ironclad. Most of the risk in the debt market falls under one of three categories:

- The issuer could default, causing you to lose your principal, not to mention all remaining interest.

- The issuer could decide to pay you back early. It's known as "calling in" or "redeeming" the debt, and it usually happens when interest rates are dropping—because the issuer can borrow "new" money more cheaply. (If you had a home mortgage at 8 percent, and rates dropped to 6 percent, wouldn't you refinance?) When securities are called in, you get your money back—but you're now forced to reinvest at lower interest rates.

- Inflation will eat away at your fixed interest rate. The stock market can often weather high inflation because companies are charging more for their goods and services. Debt holders, by contrast, are simply stuck.

Most of these risks can be mitigated, depending on how you invest. Let's take a closer look at what's out there.

Treasury securities

These are loans to the U.S. government, and they are the safest of all bonds because the U.S. government does not default on its loans. So far. That's not to say a default could *never* happen—who knows?—but the result would be the economic equivalent of global nuclear war. At the very least, a sudden lack of faith in U.S.-backed securities would plunge the world into a massive recession. The ramifications would be so serious that public and private forces all over the planet would do everything in their power to prevent it; as such, it would take some sort of epic, unthinkable dysfunctionality for a default to happen—something worse than the Great Depression, World War II, or terrorist attacks, none of which caused Treasury defaults. If you have invested in Treasury securities, you can sleep well at night.

In return for that security, you'll get a lower return than riskier investments. But Treasuries are attractive for three great reasons:

- Many are noncallable.
- Your interest can be exempt from state and local taxes (a plus if you live in a high-tax state or city).
- You can buy, sell, and manage Treasuries on a nifty government Web site called Treasury Direct without paying any broker's fees. For more information go to www.publicdebt.treas.gov.

There are five basic types of Treasury investments:

- **Treasury bills**, or T-bills, are the safest of the safe. These short-term notes are sold in $1,000 increments for terms of a few days to two years, but mostly in one, three-, and six-month terms. They don't technically pay interest but instead are sold at a discount—a $1,000 T-bill might cost you $970. When the bill matures, you get the face value. Most money market funds are invested in T-bills. In fact, putting your "rainy day" cash in a money market fund is almost the same as buying T-bills, without all the hassle.

- **Treasury notes** are intermediate securities, maturing in two to ten years. Unlike T-bills, they pay actual interest every six months. They offer rates similar to a bank CD, with no penalty for selling early. And the secondary market for T-notes is robust, so you'll have no trouble selling. If you're interested in a very safe, easy-to-manage bond investment with tax advantages, T-notes are where it's at.

- **Treasury bonds** are the long-term granddaddies, maturing in up to thirty years. If you've got that long to invest, you're generally better off putting your money in the stock market. But if interest rates are phenomenally high (and thus likely to drop), Treasury bonds can be quite lucrative since, as we mentioned, Treasury notes can be noncallable. You'll be reaping that high interest for years to come.

- **TIPS**, short for Treasury Inflation-Protected Securities, are a relatively new bond that can be a great deal because, after the first few years, the interest rate gets adjusted every six months for inflation. (It can also be downwardly adjusted in the unlikely event of deflation, but never below the face value.) The catch is that the inflation adjustment is treated as a capital gain, even if you don't realize the gain. In other words, you'll have to pay taxes every year on the theoretical uptick, even if you don't sell the bond. (Some mutual funds trade in TIPS and distribute the annual inflation gain, so at least you get what you've paid for, taxwise.)

- **Savings bonds** are not the best way to invest money, but the government has improved them in recent years. We like Series I bonds. They work sort of like TIPS, paying an inflation-adjusted interest rate. Unlike TIPS, with Series I bonds there's no tax payment until you actually redeem the bond.

  The old-fashioned EE bonds (now sold electronically) still pay an anemic interest rate, and these days you don't even get the cool engraved certificate—just a "Print Me" confirmation from your computer. The good news is, bonds redeemed for higher education costs avoid taxes, subject to some income and age restrictions. (Series I bonds also come with the education tax break.) You can also choose to pay the taxes every year—which means if you give EE bonds to a child, she can "declare" them on her own tax return (she'll owe nothing in her bracket) and redeem them tax-free later.

Mortgage-backed bonds

Here you're underwriting mortgages sold by the three quasi-governmental home lending agencies—Ginnie Mae, Fannie Mae, and Freddie Mac. They are considered rather safe, but they are also callable, and usually *do* get called in when rates drop. It's best to buy a direct mortgage-backed bond, not what's called a collateralized mortgage obligation (CMO). While CMOs pay monthly income, they carry additional risks because the maturity date can change based on interest rate changes. And with CMOs, every month you get back some principal as well as some interest. If you're not careful, it's easy to spend the principal—so when the bond matures, you've got nothing left.

Municipal bonds

You know how you step into your local voting booth and get sidetracked by that endless list of bond issues to pay for everything from a new bridge to a school gym? Here's where the money comes from. Loaning money to state and local governments is riskier than loaning to the United States, but default is still unlikely because states can't afford to alienate lenders; it would be like not paying your electric bill just before you applied for a mortgage refinance.

Our dad taught us that retired people—especially wealthy ones—love getting checks and hate paying taxes. If that's you, look no further than municipal bonds, or munis. We love munis because they are completely tax-free. Well, sort of. The interest is not subject to federal tax, or to taxes in the state and city that issued the bond. But if you live in Michigan and buy California munis, you'd still have to pay Michigan income tax on the interest. Also, if you sell the bonds at a profit before maturity, that profit is subject to capital gains tax. Overall, though, munis are a great bond investment for people in the top income-tax bracket. Look at it this way: a taxable CD paying 6 percent interest is roughly equivalent to a municipal bond paying just 4.5 percent. Hard to beat that.

Corporate bonds

Here, you are loaning money to a company. Your risk can be very small, in the case of so-called investment-grade bonds issued by highly trusted and established corporations, or very large, should you decide to invest in a freewheeling start-up. As you might imagine, the interest rate increases with the level of risk, and many corporate bonds are callable. Treasuries are safer, more liquid (meaning easier to sell), noncallable, and pay almost as much interest as investment-grade corporate bonds. If you're willing to gamble on start-ups, why not just buy stock, which gives you a piece of the company? (Corporate bonds do not generally grant an ownership stake.) If you buy corporate bonds, stick with ones that score well with the two bond rating services —garnering an A-minus or better from Standard & Poor's, or an AAA or better from Moody's.

One good thing about such corporate bonds is that, in the event of a bankruptcy, bondholders are higher in the pecking order than stockholders. That's good because you should expect corporate bonds to behave like stock—in other words, their performance is a function of the underlying stability of the company. So even very safe bonds, such as those issued by a company like General Electric, will fluctuate in value.

Convertible bonds

These corporate issues are hybrid bond/stocks, in effect, because the bond comes with an option of converting the debt into stock in the company. The advantage is that you get both the regular income of bonds and the growth potential of stocks. The disadvantage is you will probably get less of either than you would had you just bought the company's regular bonds or regular stocks. For experts who have time to work out all the details, they can be great. Our advice: leave them to the experts.

Junk bonds

One man's junk is another man's treasure. Junk bonds, known more formally as high-yield bonds, pay high interest rates but involve significant risk because the companies that issue them are new, or cash-strapped, or otherwise less than stately. They *can* be very profitable, if you know what you're doing. But let's face it: most people own bonds for safety and predictability, not a roller-coaster ride. That's what stocks are for. We tell investors to expect junk bonds to have similar volatility to stocks. And, by all means, diversify your holdings with a professionally managed fund.

Zero-coupon bonds

These bonds, issued by a corporation or government, don't pay out interest. (The word "coupon" in this context dates back to the quaint days of paper bonds, when you tore off a coupon to redeem your interest.) Instead, the monthly interest is rolled back into the bond, and the compounded return is built into the maturity price. Zero-coupon bonds can be a good deal when interest rates are high, and if you know you don't need the money for many years. Trouble is, you have to pay income tax on the interest every year, even though you don't get the money. You can avoid the tax by investing in zero-coupons through a tax-deferred IRA.

Zero-coupon bonds can provide "insurance" when matched with an equity portfolio. Let's say you have $100,000 to invest, but you can't afford under any circumstances to lose the principal.

double take

Bond Funds: Brotherly Banter

Jonathan: Mutual funds that trade bonds exist, but they don't make a lot of sense for some people. The whole point (okay, the primary point) of investing in funds is to diversify, which mitigates risk. But bonds (especially Treasuries) are less risky, so you don't really need to diversify as much. Why pay the fees? With today's bond yields as low as 4 or 5 percent, shelling out another half a percent or so in fund management fees can produce a significant erosion in return. What's more, when your money is in a bond fund you don't get a fixed interest rate (it fluctuates with the market), and you rarely profit from the maturity of individual bonds (to get your investment back, you need to sell your shares in the fund). Instead, it's generally better to simply buy bonds of varying maturities (it's called "laddering") to spread out your exposure to interest-rate fluctuations.

David: Not a bad argument, Jonathan, but I think bond funds can play an important role in your portfolio during times (like now) when even the bond market can be pretty volatile. Diversifying bond risk across a lot of issuers can be a good thing for a conservative older investor. Also, the monthly dividends from a bond fund are more flexible than those of individual bonds. For example, you can "cross-reinvest" the dividends into a stock fund within the same mutual fund family. It's a great way to build your equity position conservatively.

You could put $90,000 in zero-coupon bonds that mature at $100,000 in ten years. That way your principal is guaranteed, and you still have $10,000 left over to invest in the stock market.

THE BASICS OF ALLOCATING

The basics of *what?* Don't worry—allocating is the fancy word for that old folk wisdom that says "Don't put all your eggs in one basket." Except with your finances, if the basket falls, you lose all your retirement income. (We hate to keep mentioning those poor Enron employees who owned nothing but company stock, but their misfortune holds a valuable lesson.) Nobody, but nobody, should keep most of his assets in one *type* of stock or bond, not to mention in one company. Diversifying doesn't mean you will always come out a winner, but your chance of surviving market turmoil is much better if your money is allocated between, say, growth, income, and international stocks, plus bonds and commodities.

A Tale of Two Twins

How can diversifying help? Well, take a look at the S&P 500 index from January 1, 2001, to December 31, 2005, which increased only *0.2 percent* per year (on average) during that period. The S&P has been essentially static for five years. Except for the two-year dip from late 2001 to late 2003, the chart looks like a ruler!

So let's say that over those five years, David invests $100,000 in a mutual fund that simply tracks the S&P 500. (It's called an index fund, which we'll explain below in the section about mutual funds.) He finishes with a grand total of $102,800, including dividends reinvested. In short, he could have done much better—with far less risk—in a money market account.

Let's now assume that Jonathan takes a different path. During the same time period, he spreads his $100,000 out equally among five different investment categories: $20,000 each in the S&P 500 (remember, it tracks large American companies), the Russell 2000 Index (small companies), bonds (the Citigroup Broad Investment Grade Bond Index), international stocks (the EAFE Index), and the commodities (the Thomson U.S. Precious Metals Index). Over

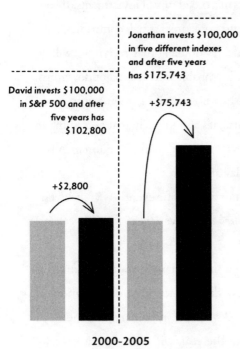

Jonathan invests $100,000 in five different indexes and after five years has $175,743

+$75,743

David invests $100,000 in S&P 500 and after five years has $102,800

+$2,800

2000-2005

the five years, that mix (including dividends reinvested) increased almost *12 percent* annually! It left the S&P in the dust. So while David watches his investments sit there (sorry, bro), Jonathan walks away with more than $175,743—nearly doubling his money. And this is during a "stagnant" market. See what a little allocating can do?

Fine, you say—but how is anybody supposed to know which areas of the economy are poised for greatness? Who'da thunk the S&P would stagnate while commodities and foreign stocks soared? The answer is, nobody can predict anything—except that as soon as you move all of your money out of the S&P 500 and into foreign stocks, you can be sure that foreign stocks will tank. Which is precisely why you need to allocate your assets in a broad mix of investments. If your money is spread out among large companies, small companies, risky stocks, and not-so-risky bonds, it's unlikely that *everything* will go belly up at the same time. You'll probably lose in a major downturn, but not as much as your cousin who put all his money into Kazakhstan energy futures. Of course, it's also unlikely that everything in your diversified portfolio will soar in a bull market—but remember, this is your retirement, not a day at the races.

Allocation, by the way, is not a one-time event. As your investments grow, it's important to *rebalance* every year, for two reasons:

David: Over the year, your investments grow (or shrink) at varying rates, which will skew the balance of your allocation. If your desired mix is 70/30 (stocks/bonds) in January, and the stock market falls 20 percent during the year, with a bond market rally

The Allocation Ballpark Number

What, you might ask, is the right asset allocation mix for moderate risk, long-term growth, and security? That depends. It depends on your age, your goals, your assets, your health, your overall comfort with risk. Many people who are confident in the long-term growth of the stock market simply divide their assets evenly into four basic mutual funds: Large-cap, mid-cap, small-cap, and foreign. That pretty much covers the equity field—although people averse to high risk would be more comfortable with some of their money in bonds.

Allocations should never be cookie-cutter plans, however, and a good financial planner will want to know a lot about you before recommending an investment strategy. But some planners suggest using a ballpark number or a quick snapshot: simply take your age as a percentage, and allocate that much of your money in more conservative investments, such as bonds, income-oriented stocks, and balanced mutual funds. For example, if you're 63, consider putting 63 percent of your portfolio into these types of conservative funds, and put the remaining 37 percent into more aggressive growth—like growth stocks, small-cap stocks, and some international equities. As you get older and closer to retirement, more of your money will get earmarked for conservative investments. This is just a rough guideline, but it can be a good tool to get you started on thinking about allocation.

of 15 percent, your mix will change accordingly. By December, your portfolio may be 60/40. It's important to ask yourself if you still have the same objective as you did back in January. If you do, get back to your desired 70/30 mix by trimming bonds and adding stocks.

Jonathan: As you get older, your allocation needs change. Young people need lots of asset growth, which entails risk; retired people need income and preservation of capital. An appropriate exposure to stocks for a young person might be 70-80 percent, whereas a retiree may only want 30-40 percent exposure to the stock market.

Likely as not, your investments will need an annual tweaking, which you can do with a phone call to your favorite advisor or mutual fund group. And, for most people, mutual funds are the best way to invest and diversify. Read on.

THE FEELING IS MUTUAL

Mutual funds are portfolios of stocks, bonds, or commodities in which investors like you can buy shares. You pay various fees (how much and how often depends on the fund, as we'll explain), and somebody else, known as a fund manager, does the work, so you don't have to pick stocks or nervously track the Dow every day. Mutual funds are the primary wealth-building investment tool you can buy, and we recommend them highly. But not all of them. Too many mutual funds perform poorly, or charge outrageously high fees, or both. In this section we'll guide you through the mutual fund maze.

Here's the deal with mutual funds, in a nutshell: in return for losing control over individual stock purchases, you gain huge diversity because every dollar you invest in a mutual fund is divided among all the investments chosen by the fund's management. That could be hundreds of companies, but more likely it's a few dozen. And even though you don't get to pick individual stocks, you have great choice in the *types* of investments that a fund chooses.

Maybe too much choice. In mid-2005, the Investment Company Institute tallied more than 8,300 U.S.-based mutual funds, with total assets of about $8 trillion. (The worldwide figures are much larger.) Personal finance magazines have turned fund-picking into a sort of fetish, with breathless headlines trumpeting the "hot" fund of the moment. At times helpful but often just noisy, their coverage can add to the confusion. To get started in mutual funds, here's what you really need to know.

The Basics of Mutual Funds

Most mutual funds are *equity funds*, also known as stock funds. But you can also buy funds that invest in real estate, commodities, or a mix of stocks and bonds. Straight bond funds, as we mentioned earlier, are not for everyone; you can buy Treasury bonds on a government Web site and avoid fees. Plus, bonds are safe so there's usually little need to diversify. (One really useful bond fund is a money market account, where you stash your rainy-day fund of three to six months' pay; it's basically a very safe T-bill mutual fund, but it's not about growth.)

Mutual funds are often grouped into *families* that are managed by one company, such as Vanguard, American, or Fidelity. The family will have many different funds, which are often designated as small-cap, mid-cap, or large-cap—a reference to the size of the companies in which the fund invests. (We explain capitalization and size in the above section on "Investing in Equity.") Besides company size, funds are distinguished in many other ways, like

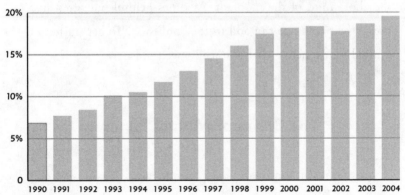

Mutual Funds' Share of Household Financial Assets

Source: Investment Company Institute and Federal Reserve Board

"growth," "growth and income," "balanced," or "income" funds. These divisions are generally related to levels of risk and return.

In personal finance seminars, we compare mutual fund investing to driving down the highway. Your goal on this journey is a big dance on the other side of the state. Assuming the posted speed limit is sixty-five miles per hour, low-risk investments like bond funds are like driving forty-five: you probably won't have an accident, but it's going to take a long time to get to the dance—and the music might be over when you finally arrive.

When you own a stock fund, on the other hand, you're cruising down the highway much faster. Stock funds fall into two basic categories: "growth and income" and "growth." Growth and income funds are typically composed of large, established, dividend-paying companies. They'll often own the most conservative (also known as "value") stocks out there. Here, you're driving sixty-five or even seventy—the upper end of the prudent speed limit, which will get you to the dance on time, albeit at greater risk of an accident or speeding ticket.

Growth funds, as their name suggests, offer capital growth as a primary investment objective. These funds seek companies and industries that are growing rapidly, and prioritize revenue growth over dividends. They're like putting the pedal to the metal and driving seventy-five or higher. You'll likely be the first to arrive at the dance—if you don't crash on the way.

Lastly, you can set your cruise control right at sixty-five by owning balanced funds (sometimes called equity income funds), which offer a mixed portfolio of stocks and bonds. Essentially, when you buy a balanced fund, you're counting on the portfolio manager to call the shots for you. Good managers will have the ability to migrate prudently between stocks and bonds, based on their particular outlook on the economy and the markets. A well-managed balanced fund can be a great compromise if you're confused about which fund is best for you.

Here's a closer look at the most common types of mutual funds, and their risk levels:

- **Aggressive growth funds** invest in fast-growing companies and are designed to maximize your return. Of course, they also entail maximum risk, so these types of funds are best for long-term investments, when you don't need the money for at least ten years. As you move into retirement, you'd want to start diversifying out of these high-risk funds. If you are in your twenties or thirties, it would be entirely appropriate to have some exposure here. Growth funds work best when you dollar-cost average into them, buying shares systematically over time. (See "Tools for the Money," p. 129, for an explanation of dollar-cost averaging.)

- **Value funds** look for good deals, based on indications we discussed earlier in our section on measuring corporate value and performance. Stocks in these funds often pay good dividends, but may not be growing as rapidly as other companies; your gain (theoretically) comes from buying in at a relatively low price. Historically, value funds do not fall as much as other stock funds when the market declines. Patience is required to be a successful value fund investor. Often, the best value stocks start out as a very unpopular investment idea.

- **Blended funds** are a mix of growth and value companies, so you get a little of both worlds. These medium-risk investments can be excellent "beginner" funds, especially if you have only a little money to start. Most mutual funds have a minimum initial investment of a few thousand dollars, which could limit your first deposit to just one fund. Choosing a blended fund gives you good early diversification, and allows the fund manager(s) to do the asset allocation for you.

- **International funds** invest, not surprisingly, in foreign companies. Besides the usual risk of market volatility, foreign investments come with the added risk of currency fluctuation and other geopolitical uncertainties —which, of course, are beyond the control of the companies you're investing in. So, yes, foreign investing is risky, but it can be highly profitable. The Japanese Nikkei stock exchange, for example, gained more than 40 percent in 2005 (after a long slide), and European stocks also saw double-digit gains during a year when American markets languished. We think just about everyone should have *some* of their mutual fund assets exposed to foreign equities. They can provide handsome potential returns, and can actually mitigate some of the risks of owning U.S. equity. (Note that in the mutual fund industry *international* means foreign, while global means both U.S. and foreign.)

- **Emerging market funds** are the riskiest of foreign investments because you're investing in companies in places like Eastern Europe, Latin America, China, and India. With currency risks, political uncertainty, and accounting "irregularities," such markets can plummet 10 or 20 percent in one day. On the other hand, good values abound in economies that have lately been growing twice as fast as the developed world. It's okay if your international fund has some exposure to emerging markets, but this should probably represent a small part of your total investment pie.

- **Exchange traded funds**, or ETFs, are index mutual funds that trade like stocks, so you can buy and sell

Dollar-Cost Averaging

Lots of people, especially the self-employed and workers who get bonuses, wait until the end of the year to transfer lump-sum savings into a mutual fund. While that's better than not saving at all, it's best to spread the same amount over the entire year, investing a little bit once a month. The reason is an investment principle called dollar-cost averaging. It's not hard to understand: by investing the same amount in the same fund every month, you benefit when share prices drop—allowing you to buy more shares for your money. When prices rise, you'll get fewer shares, so overall you will pay a lower price. If, on the other hand, you invest all of your money at once, you could lose big-time (at least in the near term) if the price drops precipitously. (To be sure, you could gain a lot if the market coincidentally starts to fly, but trying to time the market is dangerous, even for professionals.) Spreading out your stock purchases to get an average price mitigates against volatility. It's a much more prudent investment strategy than market timing—and over the long run has proven to be a very effective way to accumulate shares and build wealth.

them all day long. One advantage is that you can buy very small amounts, like a share of stock, but with far greater diversity than you would get with one share of stock. ETFs may be the fastest growing investment vehicles out there right now. They're uncommonly affordable. If you're a believer that most "active" fund managers "can't beat an index fund," look into putting together a nice portfolio of ETFs. These days, you can buy an ETF for just about every type of asset class. One problem with ETFs, like index funds, is that the fund itself is not managed by professionals. It's simply a basket of (nearly) all publicly traded securities in a specific category. While it's true that most fund managers can't beat the market, many can. Good financial advisors know who they are.

- **Sector funds** specialize in one segment of the economy—often commodities like precious metals or other "hard" assets like real estate, but also the stocks of companies in a single industry, such as telecommunications or health care. As we mentioned earlier, commodity funds are a great way to diversify beyond paper assets without having to figure out the intricacies of the gold market or managing rental properties. Be careful, though: timing is everything with sector funds.

- **Funds of funds** are mutual funds that are made up of other mutual funds. (And you thought this was going to be easy!) The advantage here is incredible diversity, since each fund in your fund has already diversified. You're also diversifying the management team and styles. The disadvantage is that management fees can be steep, since you'll be paying the fees to all the managers of all the funds in your fund. (More on fees below.) We're not big fans, due to the added layer of fees. (A fund holding various hedge funds or private equity funds may be the exception. Research carefully!)

- **Socially responsible funds** are geared to investors who want to support companies with favorable policies on a variety of concerns, such as public health, the environment, socially conscious causes, or developing nations.

- **Life cycle funds** are the flavor of the moment, reflecting the overwhelming choice in 401(k) investment plans. To simplify things, many employers and their mutual fund sponsors are offering "point-and-click" portfolios that automatically allocate depending on your age. As you get older and closer to retirement, the life cycle fund rebalances to include less risk. These funds are growing in popularity: according to a 2003 study

[*double* take]

Socially Responsible Funds

David: I think these funds are mostly malarkey. Are you trying to invest for your retirement, or make a statement? Save your opinions for the voting booth, and invest to win for your financial future. Where does it end, anyway? Is a food company socially irresponsible because it wraps products in plastic, which doesn't biodegrade? Is a retailer not allowed on the "approved" list because it has a manufacturing plant in Mexico? I can see how a few folks would be well suited for a socially responsible fund, but don't get carried away, especially if the fund's results are inferior.

Jonathan: For many people, it's not just about the money. I can see cases where people find something very empowering about socially responsible funds. Why should a cancer researcher invest her money in tobacco companies? There are also funds that follow the investing guidelines of various religions. If you have strong convictions about certain industries, don't write off these funds so quickly. A fascinating place to look for socially responsible funds is a Web site called www.socialfunds.com.

by Hewitt Associates, 55 percent of defined contribution plans offer some kind of premixed portfolio—
that's up from 35 percent in 2001. And the Investment
Company Institute says that in 2004 life cycle funds
contained some $150 billion in investments—double
the previous year.

If such funds encourage people to invest who
might otherwise throw up their hands and buy lottery
tickets, we suppose that's a good thing. But life cycle
funds are far from ideal. For starters, the managers of
these portfolios are often not very experienced; at
many companies, it's considered an entry-level
money management job. Do you really want a
stranger making important asset allocation decisions
for you? These funds seem uncomfortably imper-
sonal. Beyond that, portfolios should be about more
than your age. The forty-year-old who's been a good
saver, maxing out his 401(k) for twenty years, needs
a different investment strategy than the forty-year-old
who's starting late. (The first has a sizeable nest egg
that needs protecting, while the second needs some
very aggressive growth.) Finally, the funds don't take
into account life's surprises—such as divorce, death
of a spouse, or inheritance.

- **Load and no-load** are terms to describe whether a

fund charges a commission, or load, every time a transaction is made. The attention paid to excessive mutual fund commissions, and the "churning" of stocks to generate those fees, has given many boomers the idea that fees are the only consideration when choosing a mutual fund. Worse, some people see "no-load" and they think "free."

There is no such thing as a free mutual fund.

All mutual funds, including no-load funds, have costs associated with running them. Custodial fees, management fees (how the fund company gets paid), auditing fees, and bookkeeping fees are all part of a fund's operating expense, or overhead. In addition, many "load" funds are sold through financial advisors, who are compensated by either a sales charge (commission) or so-called 12b-1 fees (named after an SEC rule), which are often nothing more than deferred sales commissions. Where does that money come from? You, of course. Sometimes you pay an "up front" sales charge; sometimes the fee is extracted by the fund company on a "prereturn" basis.

Let's say the underlying portfolio of stocks in your fund goes up 11 percent this year. After applying the various expenses associated with running and managing the fund, you may only receive 10 percent. In this case, the "total operating expense" ratio is 1 percent. One percent of your lifetime investments can add up to tens of thousands of dollars, even for a relatively modest retirement plan. But do not be seduced into thinking that your fund is free, no matter the "no-load" come-on.

Read the prospectus! It's not terribly hard to find out the cost of a mutual fund. You can look it up on www.morningstar.com, or you can read all about it the *prospectus*, which is a fairly intimidating document that anyone can request from a mutual fund and is always provided, by law, when you invest in the fund. The prospectus will tell you, among many other things, the *expense ratio* of the fund, which is the total annual operating expense, as a percentage of net average assets. If you value the services of a broker and are not already paying for financial advice, you might not mind paying a 12b-1 fee to a broker who provides solid investment advice. Just be sure you understand what you're paying for.

Consider the turnover rate. Unfortunately, some fees are not covered in the expense ratio—notably transaction costs incurred when the fund itself buys and sells stock. Such costs can often add up to more than the "official" expenses, and the only way to get a handle on them is to look at the fund's *turnover rate*, which is also in the prospectus. A high turnover rate—say, more than 100 percent—generally means more commissions paid out by you, and more capital gains tax exposure.

The load issue looks at just one side of the mutual fund equation—cost. But the other side is performance. And like anything you buy, what you get out of it matters as much as what you pay. Read on.

The Five Ps of Mutual Funds

When financial advisors pick mutual funds for clients, we ask a lot of questions. We drill deep into the fund's historic performance, risk-taking characteristics, and holdings. Some of this information is available to you in the prospectus, but some comes in the form of "advisor-only" updates that highlight the latest developments at a fund. Good advisors will make personal visits to managers whose funds they recommend for their clients. It's all a part of due diligence—a critical step in deciding which funds to own. You can do a lot of this yourself just by poring over the prospectus and browsing Morningstar (www.morningstar.com). Here is a fund-picking guide that we call the Five Ps:

Performance. What is the fund's performance record? Harold Geneen, the late business titan who built ITT into a powerful conglomerate, once said, "In business, words are words, explanations are explanations, and promises are promises . . . only performance is reality." The best way to understand a fund's performance is to look at its track record and compare it to a *benchmark*, such as the S&P 500 for large-cap companies or the Russell 2000 Index for small-cap funds. (Index funds can also be used as benchmarks.) Don't simply look at the most recent period, which can be misleading. Instead, evaluate a variety of longer periods—say, three-year, six-year, and ten-year periods. Do what the American Funds organization does in its literature; the company goes back to the fund's inception date and highlights the average rate of return (ARR) for the best ten-year period (and when it occurred), the worst ten-year period, and the median. You should be comfortable with the *worst* performing period.

Philosophy. What is the underlying philosophy of the portfolio manager? How was his track record accomplished? Did he get lucky by making disproportionate "bets" on certain sectors, industries, or geographic locations? Is the mutual fund organization conservative or aggressive? Are the fund officers committed to doing what's best for shareholders? Does the organization seem to prioritize raising new assets and gaining market share over services for existing shareholders? The philosophies of both the individual manager and the organization should be consistent with *your* goals and objectives.

People. Who are the people responsible for the fund's track record? How experienced are they? What is their educational background? Do you trust them? Like so many business decisions, when picking a mutual fund in the end it's usually the people that matter the most. The more you can find out about them, the better off you'll be. If you're a conservative investor looking to preserve your wealth during retirement, don't buy a fund run by a gunslinging, twentysomething maverick!

(continued on next page)

(from previous page)

Process. What's the investment process within the fund? Is it managed by one person or a committee? How does a stock make it into the portfolio? Are there sell disciplines in place if a stock craters? Does the fund manager use outside research, or is the research proprietary? What's the decision-making process? How are the portfolio managers compensated? What role do company and industry analysts play, and how do they interface with portfolio managers? These overall processes should be sensible, prudent, and time-tested.

Price. What's the price? Learn what the cost is, both to purchase and to own the fund over time. Consider internal operating expenses such as custodial fees, management fees for the fund family, 12b-1 service fees, record-keeping costs, and so on. For the majority of actively managed mutual funds, the total operating expense ratio should be under 1 percent annually. Large-cap stock funds and balanced funds should be in the 0.6-0.9 percent range. Bond funds should be even less expensive. International and small-cap funds may cost a bit more.

Managed Funds and Index Funds: (Yet) Another View

Partly in response to concern over high fund fees, innovators like Jack Bogle at Vanguard pioneered the concept of index funds. Unlike funds that are actively controlled by a portfolio manager, who chooses which stocks to invest in, index funds are largely passive—the manager's job is simply to replicate a particular stock index, such as the S&P 500 or the Wilshire 5000. Without having to pay high-falutin' managers and brokers, and with very low turnover rates (stocks are bought and sold only when the index changes its roster of companies), index funds can boast extremely low fees—sometimes with expense ratios below 0.2 percent. With more of your money actually working for you, the low-priced index funds don't have to perform as well as managed funds. In addition, index funds can be very tax-efficient, because they're not burdened with having to pay capital gains distributions (upon selling portfolio holdings) the way an actively traded fund is. It's no wonder that index funds have become so popular.

The trouble with index funds is that they assume the stock market is totally random and that any investment choice will ultimately rise or fall on par with every other choice. It's like saying that, eventually, a roomful of monkeys with typewriters will accidentally bang out the collected works of Shakespeare.

Okay, but you're a boomer approaching retirement, not a monkey; how much time do you have?

We know that entire schools of financial thought are based on the concept of the random, 100 percent-efficient stock market. Proponents point to studies suggesting that, as a result, index funds often outperform managed funds (after taking fees into account). But we don't think they're always the best way to go, for a couple of reasons:

Jonathan: Saying the market is 100 percent efficient suggests that there are no discrepancies. In fact, the market is driven by all sorts of human emotions; perceptions and misperceptions abound, and a savvy manager can take advantage of those emotions—buying when others are selling, and so forth. Good portfolio managers know the market is not just a bunch of linked computers, and they can profit from the human factor.

David: When you buy an index fund, you are by definition buying every company in that index, good or bad. I don't want to own bad companies! Actively managed funds, on the other hand, own and buy companies that someone feels strongly about. They won't own the dogs. The good fund companies have research analysts who can discern the best companies from the rest. I like knowing that. As a result, actively managed funds will often outperform index funds in bear markets.

double **take**

The Financial Fee-For-All

Whomever you hire for financial advice, be careful about fee terminology. "Fee-based" is not the same as "fee only." Many stockbrokers who formerly worked just for transaction commissions are moving into fees—in part to avoid the potential for conflict of interest. When a broker gets paid a commission on the trade, it doesn't really matter if the client's portfolio gains or loses. On the other hand, when a fee-based broker works for a cut of the client's total assets—perhaps half a percent—the client's gain is also the broker's. Get the difference? But beware: fee-based brokers might also be accepting commissions from mutual funds in return for signing up clients, so even the fee-based advice might not be totally independent.

David: "Hey, JP, what's a broker get when he gives bad advice?"

Jonathan: "I don't know, what?"

David: "A commission!" (Hilarity ensues.)

David: There's a reason why fee-based financial advice has

(continued on next page)

(from previous page)

become the preferred pricing method in the investment business today. Fee-only financial advice is the most straightforward, transparent, and honest way to do business. Why? For three reasons:

1. You know exactly what you're paying. There are no hidden fees, surprise commissions, or arguments about arbitrary charges.

2. Annual fees have come down. Now, you can pay a small percentage (usually around 1 percent or so) on your total account value. So if you have one trade or 200 trades, you pay the same amount . . . and everything is included.

3. A fee-based approach aligns the financial advisor's interests with yours—namely, what he makes by managing your account is based on how well your account performs, not on how often he can buy and sell stuff. I like that. I can go to bed at night hoping that he's getting rich—because if he is, he's doing a good job for me and my family. A lot of it depends on your personality; some people are simply more comfortable paying a straight fee.

Jonathan: Good point, Dave, but let's be honest: the whole trend toward a fee-based business model is being driven not by altruistic motives, but by Wall Street's desire for a more regular income stream. Historically, investors crawl under their shells in bear markets, and transactions dry up. The fee-based model smoothes out the revenue stream for brokerage houses and planning firms. But fees may not be right for all investors. Take the "buy-and-hold" investor, who believes in owning high quality stocks and holding onto them for long periods of time. Why should he pay an ongoing fee to a planner who is simply babysitting his all-star portfolio? It would be far less expensive for that low-turnover investor to pay for each transaction, even at full-service broker commission rates. That way, the only time the investor pays is when he buys or sells a stock—and the commission is only charged on that particular transaction, not the entire portfolio.

Regulatory agencies used to worry when brokers "churned" portfolios simply to generate fees; now they're worried that fee-based advisors aren't churning enough! As a result, many fee-only advisors feel obligated to buy and sell—often to the detriment of the client—just to demonstrate that they are actively managing the account.

"SO, WHADDAYA THINK
OF THIS MARKET?"

As we finish our chapter on getting rich the prudent way, you need to know something. There isn't a day that goes by when we aren't asked about our thoughts on the market. Instead of our pontificating here on the page, let's get a bit of advice from some *real* heroes in the investment world. These gentlemen are, arguably, three of the best investment minds of all time. So let's ask them the question we all want to know, and see what they have said:

What do you think of this market?

> *When I go to a cocktail party, seven out of eight people ask me my opinion of the market. I don't usually have an opinion; I just buy good stocks and stay invested.*
>
> —Investor Peter Lynch

> *I never have an opinion on the market. The direction during the next six months is always a coin flip. What I do is to invest in good businesses, managed by good people. I buy more when other people are afraid and selling out.*
>
> —Investor Warren Buffett

Ignore fluctuations. Do not try to outguess the market.
Buy a quality portfolio and invest for the long term.

—Investor Sir John Templeton

If you ever happen to see either one of us giving a speech or delivering a presentation, ask us to show you our folder. It will contain some graphs, a note or two, a few business cards, and a copy of whatever presentation we're giving. Tucked in the very back of that folder, however, will be a wrinkled and well-worn copy of the quotes you just read. Their advice is timeless, and it has served us (and our clients) well. Honestly, folks, if these guys tell us not to focus too much on the market, we shouldn't. Period.

Chapter Six

Twins' Tips for Successful Investing

ost financial advice boils down to a few basic tenets:

- Eliminate debt, spend less, and earn more.
- Save as much as you can, and invest it.
- Let time be your ally.

There you have it. Now you can put this book down and go play tennis! In truth, very little financial advice is new and revolutionary. You've heard most of it before, possibly from your parents. So as much as we would love to reveal a radical new way to get rich quick, we can't. What we can do, however, is take the basics and overlay our own perspective and judgment. In that spirit, here are our seventeen favorite tips for successful investing.

1. Write down your plan.

There's an old saying that goes, "When you need to cut down a tree, spend 90 percent of your time sharpening the ax." Success—whether in gardening, dieting, running a business, or winning the World Series—almost always begins with a good plan. So take the time to develop your plan, and refine it regularly. These days, it's easier than ever to do what the multibillion-dollar pension and endowment funds do. They take a four-step approach to financial planning:

- Create what's known as an investment policy statement (IPS), which reflects what the organization's goals and objectives are. It describes where you are (financially), where you want to go, and how you intend to get there.

- Design an asset allocation strategy—a mix of stocks, bonds, and short-term cash instruments that can meet the goals set forth in the investment policy statement.

- Select money managers with proven track records over long periods of time, or build sensible portfolios of index funds and ETFs.

- Monitor investment results, compare them to appropriate benchmarks, and rebalance the portfolio annually.

All four of these steps are about sharpening the ax! As individual investors, we can do the same thing as the big guys, on a smaller scale. We can develop our own investment policy statement, design an appropriate asset allocation mix, hire good advisors, and monitor and rebalance.

2. Get professional help.

If you have the three Ts—time, temperament, and talent—to successfully manage your investments, go ahead and do it. That's especially true if you're just getting started. But if you have a *meaningful* nest egg saved up, children in college, and aging parents in need of care, incurring losses could complicate life for your loved ones as well as for your retirement. (Ask anyone who lost half his life's savings in the recent bear market).

Think of it this way: our parents' generation had "built-in" professional financial advice, because their pensions were managed by pros. Not only that, they didn't have to worry about who was paying the health care bill. It's different for our generation. Most of us are on our own when it comes to retirement, our kids' college, and caring for our parents. And the options have become increasingly complicated. So read this book, learn what's out there, think about your goals—and get some help that's tailored to your situation. Good financial advisors are well worth the money because they will help you to save more, get organized, stay on track, and ultimately live more securely. (See the Tools for the Money section "Getting Good Advice" on p. 153.)

3. Don't chase the hot dot.

By *hot dot*, we mean the most recent hot performer—the best mutual fund last year, or the technology stock that already jumped 100 percent. It's so tempting to point to last year's winner and say, "Why didn't I own that?" Studies have shown that the majority of fund investors purchase mutual funds at exactly the wrong time: after the fund has soared. Time after time, last year's winner will be this year's loser. There's an expression we have: "First to worst, and worst to first." In fact, investors often do better buying last year's poorer performing category than moving into last year's top performer. (In investment vernacular, this is called regression to the mean.)

It's amazing how the investment pendulum swings. During the 1980s, international stocks consistently outperformed U.S. stocks. Then, for most of the 1990s, U.S. stocks were the place to be. Now foreign stocks are flying while the U.S. market is flat. Likewise, large-cap stocks outperformed small-cap stocks from 1995 to 2001; since then, small-cap stocks have taken the lead.

You can also watch the pendulum swing between value and growth stocks. The lesson? Pay attention to the pendulum! Build up your exposure to asset classes that have lagged for the past few years, and trim from those that have outperformed.

4. Don't overdiversify.

By now most investors understand the importance of diversification as a way to mitigate risk. But some investors take it too far. Studies show that investment portfolios reach a point at which the benefit of further diversification is minimized. In fact, most benefits can be incurred by diversifying among about a dozen stocks! After that, the advantages diminish sharply, and further diversification could limit upside potential in a bull market. No less an investor than Warren Buffett believes in a concentrated portfolio. It's really based on simple math: if a stock represents just 1 percent of your portfolio, you won't gain much even if it doubles overnight. Diversified mutual funds typically own a few dozen stocks, but some have become so large that the managers are forced to buy hundreds of stocks, since rules also prohibit them from owning too much of any company. The manager might have strong convictions about forty or fifty of those companies, and the rest is mostly filler. So be careful of hugely popular funds that force you to overdiversify. By the same token, don't own shares in different funds with similar holdings.

If nothing else, this overlap increases your tax work because each fund will have a separate 1099 form.

5. Don't chase yield.

Years ago, retirees were satisfied, if not delighted, with the interest income they received from bank savings or bond investments. Unfortunately, those happy days are over. Thirty-year Treasury bonds, to cite one example, have dropped from 8 percent to about 4.5 percent. CDs suffered similar declines in rates. For people living on bond income, that's a 50 percent pay cut! Desperate to maintain their lifestyles, many retirees have turned to dicey investments like junk bonds or hybrid convertible instruments that use options and leverage to jimmy up the yield. Some of these securities are anything but—and can quickly erode your principal.

What's a smart bond investor to do? Live with today's lower yields, invest conservatively by "laddering" high-quality bonds of varying maturities, and wait for rates to rise—as indeed they are now. To learn more, visit Thornburg Investment Management's Web site at www.thornburg.com and search for *laddering*. You can also get income by buying dividend-paying stocks. See the next tip.

Getting Good Advice

Thirty years ago, our parents would see a banker for a loan, an insurance agent for life insurance, an accountant for tax preparation, and a stockbroker for investments. Today, it's hard to tell the difference between them all. Banks now boast about their private portfolio management capabilities. Stockbrokers are encouraged to write loans and sell Visa cards. Insurance agents pitch mutual funds. CPAs strategize on ways to get more than just your tax business. We have financial planners doing taxes, and lawyers hawking investment advice.

It's all about maximizing income from service fees, the new bottom line in today's competitive financial services industry. With millions of retiring boomers in need of financial management, the pickings are ripe: thousands of companies employing millions of people see the next ten years as a horse race for managing your money. Thumb through the business cards and you'll find an alphabet soup of titles:

- **FA** (Financial Advisor)
- **FC** (Financial Consultant)
- **CFP** (Certified Financial Planner)
- **CFA** (Chartered Financial Analyst)
- **CPA/PFS** (Certified Public Accountant with a Personal Finance Specialist credential)

(continued on next page)

(from previous page)

- **ChFC** (Chartered Financial Consultant)
- **CLU** (Chartered Life Underwriter)
- **CMFS** (Certified Mutual Fund Specialist)

Here's our take on whom to call when you need advice:

If you need help with your taxes: This one's easy—the *only* person you should use is a CPA. Don't let anyone else give you tax advice. Financial planners can point you in the right direction and give you tax-related information about IRA contribution limits and the like, but they should not hold themselves out as tax experts. You want to find a CPA whose only job is tax work, and who stays current on tax law—not someone who spends some of his time on taxes but also manages portfolios. For more information on CPAs, go to www.aicpa.org.

If you need legal advice: Get a lawyer experienced in whatever specialty you require. Your investment advisory firm shouldn't be preparing your legal documents. If you need estate planning, find an estate lawyer. If you need elder care work for your parents, use an elder care law specialist.

If you need financial advice: Here it really depends on the level of advice that you need. If you already have a solid budget and a good financial plan, and your investment portfolio is growing into six figures, you might be ready for an investment advisor to manage your savings. After discussing your investment goals and objectives, she'll draw up a customized investment policy statement, design an appropriate asset allocation model, search for good mutual funds, and conduct ongoing reviews and evaluations. With traditional portfolio management, total annual fees should not exceed 1.5 percent of your assets. If you have more than $1 million, don't pay more than 1 percent per year.

If you don't have a basic financial game plan, consider hiring a fee-only financial planner. He can take a look at your entire picture and get you on track to meet your goals. In general, financial planners take a more holistic approach than investment advisors, who are paid commissions and are usually more geared to making stock trades. Good planners genuinely take pleasure in helping people get financially organized.

When hiring a financial advisor, ask friends, coworkers, and family members for recommendations. Good advisors are common; great ones aren't. Try to find three likely candidates and schedule interviews with them. During the meeting, the advisor should ask you a lot of questions—not just about your finances, but also about your life goals. Are you a first-time homebuyer looking for mortgage advice, an IRA set-up, and a 529 education savings plan for your child? Do you need complex bypass trusts and estate planning? Are you heavily invested in company stock options? Do you have business succession or investment banking

(continued on next page)

(from previous page)

needs? It's important that *what you need* matches what *he is good at doing*.

You should also feel free to ask a lot of questions—including these:

1. What's your background? You want to know the advisor's education, experience, and industry certifications.

2. Do you have references? Advisors should be happy to provide pre-approved names of clients, although they should never discuss a client's financial information.

3. How often will we meet? You want to know if your advisor is reasonably available when you have questions and concerns.

4. What do you charge? These days, financial advisors shouldn't wait for you to ask. Good ones will explain their fees—and your costs—up front and clearly. And remember the expression, "if you think getting good advice is expensive, try getting bad advice."

6. Look for stable and growing dividends . . . especially if you need rising income.

One of our first TV appearances was on CNBC's *Wake Up Call*. After we bantered back and forth about the importance of dividends, anchorwoman Liz Claman dubbed us the "Dividend Duo." It's a moniker we wear proudly to this day. Dividends went out of fashion in the dot-com era, as many growth companies elected either to reinvest their cash or buy back shares. But when dot-com went "dot-bomb," the appeal of a predictable and growing dividend stream grew, as investors sought safety and stability. Today's seemingly low 3 or 4 percent dividend, compounded over time, can be an integral part of your total return, for two reasons:

- We saw earlier that reinvested dividends have accounted for a significant portion of the S&P 500 total return from 1928 to 2005. In dollar terms, an investment of $10,000 over that stretch of time would have grown to just over $700,000 without reinvesting dividends. Add them in, however, and that same $10,000 would have grown to $17 million!

- Dividends grow over time. If you need rising income (during retirement, for example), dividend-paying stocks are a good place to be these days. According to Standard & Poor's, in 2005 the number of stocks that increased the amount of their dividend payout was 9.2 percent higher than the average going back ten years. In fact, last year saw 1,949 dividend increases.

7. Invest overseas.

The majority of all publicly traded stocks are in companies based outside the United States, and half of the world's market capitalization is overseas. To ignore foreign stocks is like shopping only in aisles one through five of a ten-aisle grocery store! Foreign markets scare a lot of people, but there are tons of great companies based overseas—many trading at huge discounts compared to their American counterparts. And the potential is unlimited. China, India, and parts of Latin America have economies that are growing at about 8 percent a year. Over the next five years, China, currently the world's sixth largest economy, will build *50 million miles* of roads—as much as we currently have in the entire United States. A 2004 study by Harvard University found that if China grows at just 6 percent annually, it will overtake the United States to become the world's largest economy within the next thirty years. China's surge is the modern equivalent of the Industrial Revolution, and smart investors are paying attention. Remember: the prudent way to invest in emerging markets is through a professional money management firm that understands the inherent risks involved.

8. Don't forget hard assets.

Commodities don't get much respect, even though they are generally cheap, perform well during inflationary periods, and (as we mentioned in Chapter Five) typically cycle in opposition to stocks—so they offer protection against a volatile stock market. The year 2005 was a prime example of the need for hard assets in your portfolio. Stocks and bonds were essentially flat, with the exception of international markets, but hard assets—gold, timber, coal, steel, oil, and gas—soared.

9. Hedge against inflation.

Inflation is the enemy of financial markets. If you don't have "insurance" against the rising tide of inflation, your nest egg is in danger of drowning. Besides commodities, another great inflation hedge is Treasury Inflation Protected Securities or TIPS, as well as the government's Series I bonds. Both have adjustable interest rates that can give you sizable protection in a period of rising prices. But be careful: TIPS aren't as liquid as some other bonds, and could be harder to sell.

10. Don't try to time the market.

When you try to time the market by selling at the highs and buying at the lows, you will inevitably miss some really good trading days. So what's a few missed days? A lot! Suppose four investors each put $10,000 into the S&P 500 index for ten years, ending December 31, 2004. Now consider the following scenarios:

Investor A stays in the market all 2,519 trading days and walks away with $26,388—more than doubling her money. She is stress-free and happy, her friends commenting often that she appears mysteriously radiant, calm, and quietly confident.

Investor B tries to do a little market timing and misses only ten of the best trading days. He finishes the ten-year period with $16,451—almost 40 percent less than Investor A. His blood pressure has risen, and he's developed an unfortunate eye twitch whenever the NASDAQ drops more than 20 points.

Investor C tries even harder to time the market. Unfortunately, she misses twenty of the best market days— still less than 10 percent of all trading days in the period—and finishes with just $11,335. That's essentially break even, not counting inflation loss. She suffers from FAS—financial anxiety syndrome. She can't eat chocolate anymore without breaking out in hives.

Investor D reads all the magazine and newspapers. He's certain he knows the Next Big Thing in the stock market, and he goes in and out, following trends and whims, shifting his money this way and that. Alas, his timing is a bit off because nobody *really* knows what's going to happen next; he ends up missing thirty of the best trading days. As a result, he actually *loses* money, ending up with just $8,134 for his efforts. His obsessive-compulsive behavior over the past ten years has driven others away, including his ex-swimsuit-model wife. Now he's BAD (broke and divorced).

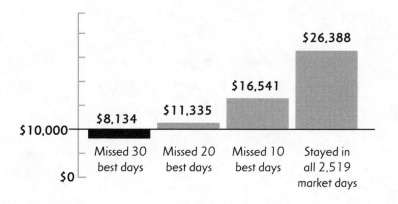

$10,000 invested for the ten years ending December 31, 2004

Clearly, the majority of the market's return comes from a very small number of days. Those days are not only rare; they are totally unpredictable. *As a result, the simplest way to reap the returns of the "best" days is to be invested during all days.*

11. Don't be prematurely conservative . . .

Too many investors make the mistake of thinking their investment horizon ends at retirement. As soon as the paychecks stop coming, they reallocate their portfolios into ultraconservative investments—forgetting that they may live another thirty or forty years, and that even average inflation *doubles* the cost of living about every twenty years. In 1984, when we graduated from college, a stamp for a first-class letter cost twenty cents; in 2006, it hit thirty-nine cents. And that's pretty tame inflation compared to that of college tuition. One year of college cost our parents $5,840 for each of us. (We had to buy our own pizza.) In 2006, our alma mater was charging a whopping $31,800 for tuition.

Every time inflation doubles, your nest egg gets cut in half. So make sure you are exposed to some growth funds, even in early retirement.

12. . . . but sometimes do nothing.

This point is related to Number Ten on market timing. Over time, the stock market has earned anywhere from 10 to 12 percent a year, depending on how you measure it. But averages can be misleading. As the saying goes, "If you place one foot on a block of ice and the other into a pit of hot coals, on average, you're comfortable." We took a look back at the actual yearly returns generated from stocks since 1929 and were surprised to see that in only two years (1993 and 2004) did the market actually return 10 percent on the money. Similarly, you'll hear about mutual funds that have averaged 10 percent per year over a ten-year period, but the actual *year-by-year* returns might look something like this:

S&P 500: January 1, 1959–December 31, 1968

1959..........12.0%	1964..........16.5%
1960 ....0.5%	1965..........12.5%
1961..........26.9%	1966.........-10.1%
1962..........-8.7%	1967 ....24.0%
1963..........22.8%	1968 ....11.1%

Average rate of return: 10.0% per year

The point is, the market sputters and languishes for periods of time that might feel interminably long, only to rebound when we least expect it. It will waffle for weeks, months, and sometimes years, doing *nothing* (like it did between 1974 and 1982), then it will surge upwards, reacting to favorable news, a surprising economic development, a positive earnings announcement—you name it.

In the words of Warren Buffett: "Sometimes, successful investing requires inactivity." One of the greatest investors of all time is telling us that the key to investing success is (occasionally) to do nothing!

And, yet, the very notion of inactivity seems counterproductive. Finance magazines and investment newsletters crow so loudly about "year-end strategies" and "quarterly rebalancing" that the pressure to do something—anything—is tremendous. Yet Buffett and other superb investors remind us not to fret so long as we own great companies, purchased at a reasonable price. Let time be your ally and sleep well tonight, knowing that a winning investment strategy may seem pretty darn boring most of the time.

13. To double your retirement portfolio, double your savings today.

A fascinating study by Putnam Investments compared the relative importance of asset allocation, mutual fund performance, and increased savings. The findings were eye-opening: increasing your savings amount from 2 percent to 4 percent of your income yielded a far greater return over fifteen years than being in the best mutual funds or picking a more aggressive allocation. The study, which looked at the period of January 1, 1990, to December 31, 2004, found that investors who owned shares in the top-performing mutual funds gained only 6 percent over those in the worst-performing funds. A more aggressive asset allocation increased return by 20 percent. But doubling the savings rate (from 2 to 4 percent) had ninety times the impact of being in better funds! The lesson here is that, over the long term, obsessing over which fund, or how much money to put into growth stocks, matters little compared to how much you save.

14. Play good defense.

Growing up in Pittsburgh in the 1970s, we worshipped the Steelers football team. Despite the fame of offensive stars like Bradshaw, Swann, Stallworth, and Harris, it was the Steelers' defense—the Steel Curtain—that led the team to four Super Bowl victories. Offense may get the glory, but good defense wins ballgames.

It's the same with investing. Good defense will keep you in the game. If there was one lesson from the bear market of 2000-2002, it was the importance of having downside protection. Retirees in particular learned how difficult it can be to recover from investment loss. Here's why: if you lose money in one year, it takes disproportionately more the next year to get back on track. Let's say you want to average a 10 percent return annually. Here's how it looks with a $100 investment:

Year 1	Year 2	Year 3	Year 4	Year 5
$110	$121	$133	$146	$161
+10%	+10%	+10%	+10%	+10%

But let's say you hit a pothole in Year Four and *lose* 20% of your money:

Year 1	Year 2	Year 3	Year 4	Year 5
$110	$121	$133	$106	$161
+10%	+10%	+10%	-20%	+52%

As you can see, in order to get back to your original goal of 10 percent annualized return in Year Five, you'd need to earn more than 50 percent. Even in a spectacular economic environment, such a one-year return is nearly impossible.

So what's the solution? Well, one of them is to reduce your fourth-year loss. If, for example, you only lost 10 percent in year four, here's how it would look:

Year 1	Year 2	Year 3	Year 4	Year 5
$110	$121	$133	$120	$161
+10%	+10%	+10%	-10%	+<u>35</u>%

Or, better yet, look at the results if we can keep our fourth-year loss to zero:

Year 1	Year 2	Year 3	Year 4	Year 5
$110	$121	$133	$133	$161
+10%	+10%	+10%	0%	+<u>21</u>%

Basic math illustrates that if you can limit (but not necessarily avoid) losses in Year Four, long-term investment success will be easier to attain, because you won't have to swing for the fences in Year Five. To do that requires teamwork: mixing offensive *wealth-growers* like stocks with defensive *wealth-preservers* like income stocks, bonds, hard assets, and a little cash.

15. Be a value investor.

Many of the world's most successful investors—including Warren Buffett, Benjamin Graham (author of the classic book *The Intelligent Investor*), Bill Miller, Sir John Templeton, and Jonathan Bell Lovelace—got that way by looking for value. In a nutshell, they believe that the daily ups and downs of the stock

market present constant opportunities to buy into good companies at less than their fundamental value. The reason is that stock
prices don't always correspond to what's *really* happening at a
company—a lot of human emotion, much of it in the category
of overreaction, drives the market. As a result, good deals abound
if you care to look for them.

There are thousands of good companies out there to invest in.
But if you pay too much, you won't make money. In the end,
value investing is about two exercises:

- Identifying great companies.
- Determining a fair price to pay, relative to the company's intrinsic value.

Most people don't have the time or knowledge to shop for
value stocks like the big investors do, but you can invest in value
stock funds that are managed by people who do.

16. Invest every month.

When you invest every month (like you do in a 401(k) plan),
you are insulated from market fluctuations because over time you
will be paying the average price for stock. As we mentioned in
Chapter Five, so-called dollar-cost averaging really works—
except when the market is shooting straight up, day in and day

out, without fluctuating. (In that case, you would be better off having put all your money in at the very beginning of the run-up.) But that's about as likely as snow in San Diego. Here's how regular investing trumps market timing.

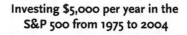

Investing $5,000 per year in the S&P 500 from 1975 to 2004

$1,390,907 — 12% annual return — Worst day (market high)

$1,675,263 — 13% annual return — First day of each year

$1,751,392 — 13.5% annual return — Best day (market low)

17. Asset Allocation: Building the Right Portfolio for You and Your Family

When a CNBC interviewer asks us to recommend the "ideal asset allocation in today's environment," it's never an easy question to answer. Not because of the environment, but because of the person for whom the asset allocation is designed. That's why we have to laugh a little when some pundits seem eager to make a blanket statement like "In today's market, investors should be in sixty-five percent stocks, twenty-five percent bonds, and ten percent cash." It's a little like asking a doctor, "What should I take for a splitting headache and occasional dizziness?" Well, it depends on the diagnosis, doesn't it?

The same goes for recommending an asset allocation for you and your family. Whether you have 35 percent or 85 percent of your portfolio in stocks is a function of your age, your background, what you need the money to do for you, how much risk you're willing to tolerate, your previous investment experience, and other important factors that may affect your financial well-being. Only with that knowledge can anyone make a recommendation that's suitable for you. Here's what some asset allocation models look like. Make sure to customize one that is appropriate for you.

Examples of Asset Allocation

Conservative Portfolio

Moderate-Conservative Portfolio

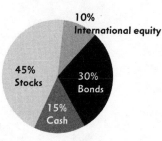

Moderate Portfolio

Moderate-Aggressive Portfolio

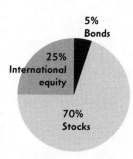

Aggressive Portfolio

Chapter Seven

The New Retirement

You see, I wanted to sing gospel, but I wanted to make me some money, too.

—Soul singer Wilson Pickett

Meet Steve, an old friend and colleague of ours. Steve, now 61, has been retired for four years, after a thirty-four-year career in financial services. He's a divorced father of three grown children, and he's been dating the same woman for many years. Thanks to his investments and a pension (he worked for the same company almost his entire career), he's financially comfortable but not without worries: his ninety-one-year-old mother, who has virtually no assets of her own, recently became ill and is now in a nursing home. Meanwhile, the property tax on his large Seattle home has skyrocketed. He also owns a beach house in Oregon, which he is unwilling to give up because he loves the water. In fact, he'd happily move there full-time, but he needs to be near his mom in Seattle.

Overall, Steve feels very fortunate. "I grew up dirt poor," he says, "and I've been working as long as I can remember. I had three paper routes by the time I was ten. I was lucky enough to get into a good business and do quite well."

But as happens to so many of us, not everything went according to plan for Steve. His retirement was sudden and involuntary, thanks to poor health—the cumulative toll on his body, especially his back, from a lifetime of car accidents, high-speed boating accidents, and, incredibly, getting crushed in the door of a Boeing 727 that blew shut from a jet blast.

None of those accidents matched the trauma of an unplanned retirement.

"My work was my passion," Steve says. "I loved helping people figure out their future—and one day, all of a sudden, my own future just got zapped. I didn't expect to go out this way. The New York stock markets open at 6:30 in the morning out here in Seattle, and for a long time I would get up early and check the markets, like I was still working."

That was four years ago. Since then, Steve has come to terms with his new life, made significant adjustments, and learned a lot in the process. We'll be checking back with Steve later in the chapter, because his story resonates with so many of us.

It's not surprising that boomers, who questioned traditional models at every stage of life, are now seeking new definitions for retirement. The old model of a black-and-white separation between work and leisure is no longer valid. We see this not just in retirement: look at the increasingly popular "job sharing" schedules, which allow an employee to share one job with another person (making more time for family) or telecommuting (again, more time at home, less time in traffic). Look at the home office, a must-have room in the fashionable boomer house. (Mahogany built-in desks optional.) These trends are all blurring the distinction between work and play, office and home, job and family.

Retirement is changing along with the overall labor model. Get this:

- According to AARP/Towers Perrin, 68 percent of older workers plan to work beyond retirement—or never retire at all.

- About 7 million previously retired Americans have returned to work.

- In 2005, the number of workers aged sixty-five to seventy-four grew at *triple* the rate of the total workforce.

- The Bureau of Labor Statistics reports that more than *22 percent* of Americans age sixty-five to seventy-four are working. That's up from just 15 percent twenty years ago.

But the nature of their work is changing. Many have quit their formal jobs earlier than the traditional age of sixty-five, only to take up a new career, start a business, or devote time to volunteer work.

And retirees who do stop work altogether probably won't be seen around the shuffleboard court. They'd rather be hiking, or skiing—or riding a Harley across Alaska. Better health means more active seniors, at work and play. Seniors who are out there in the world will also be spending money—and savvy marketers are poised to grab a piece of that business. We wrote earlier about the fact that boomers are the most media-saturated generation in history; don't expect that to change as we age!

Mostly what's changing is the way we *think* about retirement, driven by a few positive dynamics:

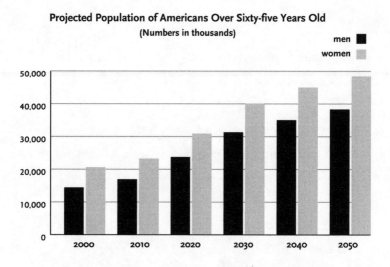

Projected Population of Americans Over Sixty-five Years Old
(Numbers in thousands)

Source: U.S. Census Bureau, 2004, "U.S. Interim Projections by Age, Sex, Race, and Hispanic Origin"

- **Longevity.** As we've seen, it's entirely possible that boomers will live a quarter century or more after turning in the keys to the office. That's a lot of golf! Yes, we know people who could and would play golf every day for twenty-five years—but many other retirees find themselves longing for something else to balance their well-deserved leisure activities.

Additional life expectancy after age sixty-five
(based on year in which person turns sixty-five)

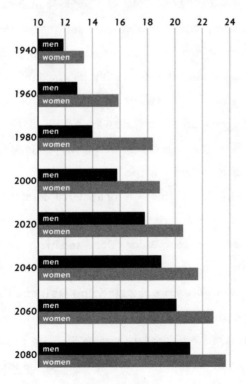

Source: Social Security Administration

- **Better health.** Besides living longer, people are living better, which makes them more able to work. Another way to put it is that people are living longer without necessarily "growing older." To cite just one example, a previously crippling but nonfatal ailment like arthritis can now be largely controlled. As a result, more of us are able—and eager—to work well into our seventies.

- **The "give-back" bonus.** Nate worked for a major software manufacturer after college, and then founded his own very successful company. By the age of forty, he was a multimillionaire with a big, paid-off house and a great family. It was a perfect picture, with just one nagging problem: Nate wasn't fulfilled. "When my wife and I were in college we spent a year in Africa," he recalled, "and I learned how people can get by with very little in the way of material comfort. I'll never forget that experience. I decided back then that I wanted to move to Walden Pond and live in a cabin like Thoreau—you know, the simple life. Well, it's been twenty-five years since then, my life is crazy, and I have more material possessions than anyone deserves. So much for the simple life!" He paused: "It's funny, though. The yearning I had for the simple life? It's still there . . . like this quiet voice that calls

me when I'm alone somewhere . . . one of these days,
one of these days. . . ."

Few of us are as financially blessed as Nate, but versions of his
story are common among boomers, who grew up in a period of
sweeping idealism only to settle into a middle age of hypermaterialism. After years of getting and spending, many of us are ready
to give something back—perhaps to reclaim the idealism of our
youth. The pattern can go something like this:

Sweeping idealism of youth

Hypermaterialism in middle age

Happiness, fulfillment, and meaning
in our lives during retirement

Nate admits that he will probably never live in that one-room
cabin, but when he retires, he plans to start a new company—this
one designed to help young entrepreneurs start retail businesses
in Africa.

At this point you may be saying, "Do you guys live in a
vacuum?! What about the *negative* dynamics that are forcing
retirees back to work—like frozen pensions, skyrocketing health

care costs, and an anemic stock market?" It's true. Most retirees work because they need the money.

In fact, a 2003 survey conducted by AARP found that the most common reason for postretirement employment was a need for money, followed by concern over rising health care costs. But this shouldn't be surprising: ask anyone why he goes to work every morning and the answer will almost certainly be "I need the money" or "I need the benefits"—even if he loves his job. Since when did needing money preclude enjoying work? Most people get at least

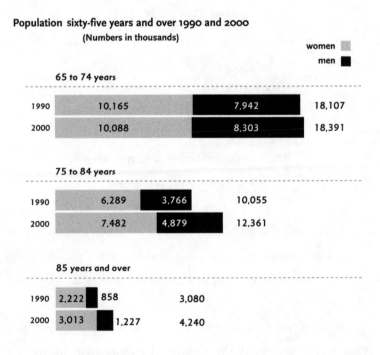

Population sixty-five years and over 1990 and 2000
(Numbers in thousands)

women
men

65 to 74 years

	women	men	total
1990	10,165	7,942	18,107
2000	10,088	8,303	18,391

75 to 84 years

	women	men	total
1990	6,289	3,766	10,055
2000	7,482	4,879	12,361

85 years and over

	women	men	total
1990	2,222	858	3,080
2000	3,013	1,227	4,240

Source: U.S. Census Bureau, Census 2000 Summary File;
1990 Census of Population, *General Population Characteristics, United States* (1990 CP-1-1)

some satisfaction out of their jobs, even if the primary objective is keeping the wolf at bay. Retirement today might include work out of necessity, but it's also a chance to push your reset button.

Like just about everything else today, it's not a retirement that our grandparents would recognize. Yet oddly enough, it might have made perfect sense to *their* grandparents.

A NEW MODEL FOR RETIREMENT

We tend to think of the old model of retirement—working until age sixty-five, followed by a few years noodling around the house and collecting benefits, then death—as a long-standing tradition. In fact, the whole idea of formal retirement is a fairly new concept. It began in the early twentieth century, when burgeoning industries decided that aging employees were less productive than the youngsters lined up to start their own careers. Institutionalizing retirement made room for new workers, and was not a distasteful concept to labor unions, either. Before then, people mostly worked until they got too sick, then were cared for by their children until death. (Farmers, who made up most of the population in the nineteenth century, simply worked until they died.)

Trouble was, what to do with all those newly retired workers? How would they live? Some had pensions and caring families, but what about those who didn't? The solution, of course, was Social Security, enacted in 1935 as a way to lift retirees—we're talking

The Five Traps of Early Retirement

1. The Social Security catch.

You're allowed to start drawing Social Security checks as early as age sixty-two. But if you do, you'll get lower payments for the rest of your life—depending on when you were born, as little as 70 percent of your full eligibility. Not only that, if you also work, your income could reduce your payments even further. Waiting until the full-benefit age of sixty-five to sixty-seven (depending on when you were born) will net you more cash annually, and at that point any income will not affect benefits. Even so, the average age when people begin drawing Social Security is sixty-three. If you can afford to hold off, do so.

2. The investment drain.

Thanks to compounding, your lifetime investments are earning the most money at the very end—just before you start withdrawing for retirement income. Start those withdrawals earlier and you'll reduce the power of your savings. The longer you can leave your nest egg invested, the better.

3. The separation strain (where'd my job go?).

Don't confuse lack of fulfillment with working in general. Many people look forward to early retirement, then realize after a couple of years that what fulfilled them was work. Some try to reenter the workforce—but, it's not so easy.

4. The health care snare.

If you retire before Medicare kicks in, you could find yourself in limbo when it comes to health insurance. You can sign up for coverage under COBRA, which requires your previous employer to keep you enrolled, but it's very expensive. And if you or your spouse has any preexisting health conditions, it can be hard to get private insurance. (State laws vary on this topic.)

5. The home-front headache.

Early retirement can cause a lot of marital stress—usually when a husband is ready to quit but his wife isn't ready to have him around the house twenty-four-seven. How can she tell him to keep working for three more years when he's sick and tired of the grind? How do they keep from getting on each other's nerves? This is where advance planning and good communication can really make a difference. One newly retired couple we heard about breaks their week into "my time" and "our time." On Mondays, Tuesdays, and Wednesdays, she goes to lunch with friends, plays cards, and sets up tennis matches. Meanwhile, he'll golf, work on family finances, and enjoy going out for an occasional dinner with a friend. On Thursdays, Fridays, and Saturdays, they do things together—visit a gallery or museum, see a show, or visit family. This compromise has been an effective way for them to maintain their own identities and a sense of independence.

about everybody's parents, after all—out of abject poverty. The program was wildly successful based on that initial objective: today, seniors are the most affluent of Americans, overall.

Now, though, things are far less certain for those of us approaching our later years. For starters, the idea of automatically retiring when the clock strikes sixty-five is under assault. In that sense you could say we've come full circle, back to the days before formal retirement, albeit with some new twists. Very few of us have pensions that provide a guaranteed check in the mail until we die. Instead we have "do-it-yourself" retirement plans like 401(k)s and IRAs that—combined with Social Security stipends—may or may not keep us going. It's the "may not" part that adds a lot of stress and uncertainty, but it also gives us more choice. And *that's* the key: you want to define your retirement based on choice, not desperation.

The way to do that, like anything else, is through careful planning. The buzz phrase in money management circles today is *life planning*, as opposed to the myopic old *financial planning*. From our standpoint, there is very little distinction between the two terms; it's all part of the same goal. In our own work, we see that clients who have made sound financial decisions—living within their means, saving regularly, and taking prudent risks with investments—are most likely to think creatively about life after retirement. It only makes sense: if you're worried about where the money is coming from, it's hard to think about anything else. But if you feel relatively secure financially, you're able to step out of that "money bubble" and view the world from a wider perspective.

In previous chapters we outlined how to set financial goals and keep them on track. Now, it's time for the next step—combining your good financial habits with sound "life" preparation.

Jonathan: I think retirement is really a time of great optimism and fulfillment. In retirement, we have an opportunity to clean the slate and reinvent ourselves, and that can be empowering and liberating. You can spend more time with your spouse and family, take up new (or old) hobbies, start a new business—whatever motivates you.

David: I'm a big fan of Ken Dychtwald, the gerontologist and author of *Age Power*. He believes that the key to retirement happiness is not just money but engagement with the world, intellectual stimulation, and *how* you face both physical and mental challenges. He says that when we reach our fifties and sixties, we need to see ourselves as entering the next chapter of life. It's not "the beginning of the end of life," as he puts it, but a positive, fulfilling, and even fun time. Unfortunately, life's surprises can sometimes throw a wrench into our retirement plans. If that happens, however, preparation can make all the difference.

INVOLUNTARY RETIREMENT—AND HOW TO PREPARE FOR IT

We saw how Steve had to retire early due to poor health—the second most common reason, after corporate downsizing, for involuntary retirement. When work ends before you're ready to quit, it can be a real shocker. Yet considering how often it happens, few people seem prepared.

If you're in your fifties or sixties and you get downsized out of a job, your first reaction is to hit the pavement and find another job, quickly. Fair enough—chances are good you need the money—but what happens next can be frustrating. You'll likely be interviewed by a potential boss who is much younger than you, perhaps younger than one of your kids—an "echo boomer" or even (yikes!) a Generation Y baby. This tyke of a titan might not come right out and say it, but lots of people are uncomfortable giving orders to someone who could have changed their diapers. They might also wonder if you will take kindly to their suggestions; after all, you've done it your way for a long time. And what about technology? Are you up on the latest software, or the coolest tools? If your job is physical, there could be health concerns.

"No one comes out and says you're too old," says Dennis (not his real name), a sixty-year-old client of Jonathan's who lost his job as head of the ad sales department at a major TV station. "They say you're

Percentage of Americans fifty-five and older as share of workforce

1984	1994	2004	2014
13.1%	11.9%	15.6%	21.2%

Source: Bureau of Labor Statistics

overqualified. I'd love to try working in a different field, and I think I could do well, but then they say I'm underqualified. Basically, they don't want to give you the opportunity if they perceive you as being old. But I'm not ready to be put out to pasture."

Dennis has been looking for work for six months while doing consulting jobs. Although his wife doesn't work, at least their two kids are out of college, "so that expense is behind me," he says. Nor does he worry about aging parents: "My mother passed away a few years ago, and my dad is in great health at age ninety-one. I'm not destitute, but I'm not worry-free either. But it's been a humbling experience. Like a lot of people, I lost money in 2000 and 2001. If I still had that, I'd be fine."

Studies suggest Dennis is not alone. According to the Bureau of Labor Statistics, in 2004 displaced older workers needed an average of 25.8 weeks—half a year—to find a new job, compared to 18.9 weeks for younger workers. Even if you can't predict late-career job loss, you can take these six steps while you're employed to make the shift easier—if you lose your job.

1. Buy disability insurance.

If you are no longer able to work due to an accident or illness, you'll get some money from Social Security (provided you meet their strict guidelines, designed to counter rampant disability fraud), but not nearly enough. And you might have disability insurance through your job. Otherwise, you should buy a private policy. Depending on your age and health, disability insurance can be expensive—much more than life insurance, in part because injuries are more likely than early death. Still, it's worth it. "In hindsight, I wish I had bought disability insurance," says our friend Steve. Look for a policy that pays at least 75 percent of your income (it's called residual benefits). And you want "owner's occupation" coverage—meaning you're covered if you cannot perform your current occupation. That way, if an eye injury ends your career as a commercial airline pilot, you won't have to work as a warehouse clerk. Another good option is a cost-of-living adjustment that accounts for inflation.

2. Save plenty for emergencies.

"They tell you to have three to six months of living expenses in an emergency fund," says Dennis. "After looking for a job for the past six months, I'd recommend nine to twelve months."

3. Stay on top of trends.

Knowing the latest computer technology and other work-related trends can help if you need to find other work. Take this test: when something goes haywire on your office computer, do you immediately phone Tech Support, then go out and grab a latte, or do you try to work through the glitch yourself? If your answer is "make it a double with extra foam and cinnamon," consider upgrading your tech savvy. Many large companies offer free training seminars in computers and other technology.

4. Be flexible.

In almost every job there are opportunities to learn a new skill; seek them out, so if you need to make a fast change you'll have a broader knowledge base. Make it a goal to understand every aspect of your company. Don't be like Freddie Prinze in *Chico and the Man*, whose famous rejoinder to any request was, "It's not my yob, man!" Instead, be like the billionaire media mogul and DreamWorks cofounder David Geffen, who famously began his career in the mailroom of a talent agency, then learned everything about the entertainment business from the ground up.

5. Cultivate relationships.

Lots of professionals assume they can sail into semiretirement as a consultant in their previous field. But the number of people who actually make consulting pay off is much smaller than you'd think. Those who succeed have typically done the spade work—spending years cultivating business relationships, and not just with coworkers. A good way to meet colleagues is through trade groups and other work-related organizations. Lastly, create a file called "important contacts." Start writing down the names of people you've met over the years who are influential: people you worked with, longtime friends, mentors, favorite clients, family members, etc. You'll be amazed at the number of influential people you know. If you have (or had) a good relationship with them, believe us, they'll be delighted to hear from you, and happy to offer some advice if you need it. As time goes by, continue to add new names and/or business cards to your list.

6. Invest in a business opportunity.

AARP says that one in six retirees will start her own business. Smart ones begin that process while they're still working. In fact, owning his own business was a major boost for Steve. Eighteen years ago, he bought a small company that makes bacterial enzymes used to enhance the performance of sewage treatment plants. "I bought it as part of my plan for retirement," says Steve. "These days I oversee it, but I'm not actively involved. Still, it keeps me in the business world, and it allows me to meet new people."

Even if you never face involuntary retirement, preparing for the possibility will give you peace of mind—and it will serve as a fail-safe as you lay the groundwork for other retirement options that you actually choose.

VOLUNTARY RETIREMENT—AND HOW TO GET THERE FROM HERE

Many of our clients are retired. So we see firsthand that voluntary retirement is much better than the alternative! People who have planned for the next phase in their life—with their heart, mind, and hands, as well as their mutual funds—are happier, healthier, and in every way more vibrant.

Even so, it can be hard for people to look beyond their investment portfolio. Here's what typically happens in a life-planning session with a new client:

David (playing the part of the financial advisor): So, Jonathan, when you close your eyes and dream of your retirement, what do you see?

Jonathan (playing the new client, eyes closed): Golf!

David: Wow, that's a new one. Just kidding! What else? Let me guess . . .

Jonathan and David (in unison): Travel!

David: I must be clairvoyant. Now answer me this: What do you plan to do when you come back from that Mediterranean cruise?

Jonathan: Ummm . . . golf!?

David: Pretend it's raining. Seriously, think about your past interests and activities away from work.

Jonathan: Well . . . hmmm . . . Now that you mention it, years ago I used to help teach adult literacy in a program through my church. I've always loved to read, and I enjoyed helping other people to learn. But then life got in the way; between my job and my family, there was no extra time. (*Thoughtful pause.*) I guess I'd like to get back into that. In fact, just the other day I saw a write-up in the paper about the surprising number of illiterate adults right here. They're usually too embarrassed to admit it, but lots of them do try to get help, and they need volunteers.

David: Sounds like you'd be a huge asset to the program, even for just a few evenings a month. What a great way to give back to your community. But what about your own personal development? I mean, a few months of travel, a bit of golf, some volunteer work—is that enough to keep you busy? You're looking at years, maybe decades, of good health. What makes up for going into work everyday?

Jonathan: I hear you. The truth is, my wife is wondering the same thing. I mean, she's got all kinds of clubs and activities to keep her busy. The more I think about it, some kind of work might be a good thing—and the money couldn't hurt our bottom line, either. I've actually thought about being a fishing guide. I've paddled just about every lake and stream in the state, going way back with my own dad; if I spent a few summers boning up before retirement, I bet I could pass the guide test blindfolded, and I already own all the equipment. While I've still got my health, I could make a nice little income every summer, and have a blast too. Most of the clients would be retired guys like me, so we'd have a lot in common. Getting paid to fish could even be better than golf.

David: What're you waiting for? You've got people to teach and fish to catch!

You can see where we're headed. When most people daydream about their retirement, they tend to think of the obvious—those leisure activities that seem to happen so rarely in a working life. But when you get people thinking harder about their own lives, and looking at the big picture, all sorts of dreams and aspirations crop up. Now may be the time to actually listen to those quieter voices, because your retirement days have the same twenty-four hours as any other day. How will you occupy them?

People who think retirement is about quitting a dead-end job are likely to be disappointed when the big day arrives. The best solution to a bad job is finding a better job, not counting the days to retirement. We've found that people who spend their careers in unchallenging work, never making an effort to change, probably identify with their job on some basic level. So when retirement comes, they are lost. They haven't tilled their garden, so to speak, in years, then they're surprised when nothing grows.

Of course, people who love their jobs can be at even greater risk for separation anxiety. When your job is your life, what comes next? We know a man named Jim who was deeply hurt when his twenty-four-year-old son confessed that he hadn't found time to watch a video of his father's retirement party. Jim had founded a small midwestern advertising agency that grew over the years into one of the largest in the state; his retirement was a huge bash, with dozens of testimonials, one after another. When Jim finally confronted his son with his disappointment, the son was shocked. He admitted that he hadn't considered how important it was to his dad. "I can understand how much your career meant to *you*," he told his dad. "But to *me*, you're the guy who knew how to fly a kite."

Nobody at the retirement bash had praised Jim for his kite flying.

Often people don't realize how much of their life is defined by work. While it's possible to meet best friends, soul mates, and even a spouse on the job, many of your work relationships are more shallow and will dissolve quickly in retirement. (It's amazing how many work "friends" you'll rarely hear from once you retire!) Taking steps in advance to develop your life away from work will help ease the transition—and make you a fuller person today. We collected the following ideas from a few retired friends of ours:

Six keys for a smooth transition into retirement

- **Plan first.** While two-thirds of retirees are living the lifestyle they hoped for, more than half "wish they had planned differently" in their final working years, according to a recent retirement study conducted by Fidelity. Amazingly, two-thirds of those polled said they had not completed a budget for their retirement years, and 75 percent didn't have an asset allocation strategy.

- **Seek out friends away from work.** It's healthy to have a broad range of relationships outside of your career. Obvious places to make friends include your church and around the neighborhood. If your best friends are mainly from work, keep the "shop talk" to a minimum and focus on your other interests, like sports or hobbies. "I'm lucky to have a close network of friends," says Steve. "A few of us share a love of old British sports cars, and we go to car shows together. That's been a big help in the transition."

- **Hobbies can save your life.** Julia has been a passionate amateur photographer since childhood, and retirement has given her the time to pursue her hobby with relish—especially the new frontier of digital photography. "I see so many retirees who have no hobbies or passions—nothing going on in their life," she says. "I may be crazy, but they're the ones who seem to die early!" (She wasn't kidding.)

• **Reconnect with your spiritual side.** Lots of people find that their careers distracted them from spiritual development. We hear that retirement can be a great opportunity to rekindle that flame. Whether it's meditation classes or getting more involved in your church or synagogue, replenishing your spirit can be uplifting. A minister of David's once said, "We all have a God-shaped hole in our heart that cannot be filled with anything else."

• **Volunteer!** Before he retired, Steve spent years volunteering as a reserve officer for the local sheriff's department. Now he donates his time to a county agency that serves the mentally disabled. "That's been very rewarding," he says. "Helping others is also a constant reminder how fortunate I am."

• **Rent an office.** If you plan on doing some form of retirement work that's different from your current job,

having a separate office well in advance can help
define your new identity. Some people dedicate space
in their home to a retirement office, but many couples
find it's better to have a little more separation at the
beginning. You can always change your mind later.

Many studies have shown that people who retire *later* are happier than those who cut out early—perhaps because they have
given more thought to the process. And the really great thing
about late retirement is that it takes a lot of the pressure off your
finances. Just a few more years of saving and investing can make
all the difference.

Let's say you have $500,000 in retirement savings at age sixty-
two. By working five more years and socking away $1,000 a
month, you'll retire at age sixty-
seven with $710,000, assuming a
conservative 5 percent annual gain.
You'll earn $150,000 in interest
alone. Imagine if you had invested
a million dollars, in a strong
market! Plus, at that age, you'll be
eligible for full Social Security benefits. These additional savings will
help cover assisted living or nursing
home expenses down the road.
Although the average annual cost

**Work five more years and
get $10,500 more per year**

work just five
more years
and retire at
67 with
$710,000

retire at 62
with
$500,000

$35,500/year

$25,000/year

of assisted living is $30,000 ($60,000 for nursing homes), when asked what source they would use to pay the bulk of long-term care costs, 31 percent of respondents in a study by MetLife listed Medicare, health insurance, or disability insurance—none of which actually cover the cost of long-term care.

If you can't bear the thought of working five more years, try to "compartmentalize" the time, and think in stages:

- **Pre-retirement.** In this stage you're still in the full-time workforce, getting health insurance and other benefits, but you might be working more from home while planning for the next stage. This is a time to be developing contacts and formulating interesting ideas, should you be planning on a second career. Also, if you're over age fifty, be sure to take advantage of "catch-up contributions," which allow you to put thousands of additional dollars into your IRA ($1,000 more) or 401(k) ($5,000 more) for 2006.

- **Early retirement.** This period marks your departure from formal full-time employment, though perhaps you continue to do part-time work in your field, as well as volunteer work. It's also a time to be setting off on any new career paths. You're building in plenty of time for family and leisure activities. Financially, you enjoy a modest income and (ideally) health benefits.

- **Late retirement.** You've stopped working for income altogether, living entirely off your investments, pensions, and Social Security. You're enjoying travel, reading, and volunteer work. One great source of pride is your grandchildren, whose educations you are helping to finance.

Sounds great, doesn't it? By now you might be thinking, how do I make that work if I haven't saved quite so diligently? Am I destined to live in a welfare hotel? Not at all. The fact is, most Americans have not saved enough for their ideal retirement. That's one reason why so many "retirees" keep working. But there are other ways to make ends meet in retirement. Here are our favorites:

MAKING ENDS (AND NEW BEGINNINGS) MEET: SIX WAYS TO MAKE YOUR MONEY LAST A LIFETIME

1. Stop paying for life insurance.

By retirement you should be self-insured, which means you and your spouse have enough assets to support the other in the event one of you dies. Life insurance is meant to replace your income, but once you're no longer working, it may be moot. Review the choices with an insurance expert, but don't put too much pressure on yourself to leave your children a ton of dough. You are not a lottery ticket.

2. Downsize your house.

You can save a bundle by moving to a smaller house. Even if your mortgage is paid off, property taxes and maintenance costs on a big house can put a major crimp in your budget. Just ask our friend Steve, who finally sold his big house in Seattle for a much smaller place: "My house was becoming a cash drain. Property tax was up to $1,600 a month, the gardener was $600 a month, insurance was another $300. All that added up to three times the mortgage." Some retirees rationalize keeping a big house so the kids have a place to stay. But unless your children are moving back home, you'd be better off putting them up in a local B&B during the holidays rather than paying the year-round costs of maintaining that large home. Oh, and if you buy a cozy smaller home? Call it a bungalow: your architect friends will be impressed!

3. Move to a cheaper community.

Lots of prospective retirees talk about relocating to a cheaper town, perhaps in a sunnier climate, but the reality is that very few

Getting By on Less—or Not?

David: Sometimes people who retire early have incorrect assumptions about expenses. It's often suggested that during retirement you'll need 70 or 80 percent of your current income. But if you're only in your late fifties and planning to travel, eat out, join a club or two, and pay for your own health care, you could easily outspend your current lifestyle. Recent retirees are surprised, for example, at how much more money they spend during the week, simply because they have more time on their hands. As a result, early retirees should probably count on needing *all* of their current income.

Jonathan: Good advice, but not for everyone. If your kids are out of college and your house is paid off, you've got two major life expenses out of the way. Groceries eat up a ton of money, no pun intended, and with the kids gone you'll save a lot there, too. Cut out commuting costs, work clothes, dry cleaning—the list could go on and on. I think lots of early retirees really *can* get by on less than their current income. It all depends on your choices.

actually make the move. There's family to consider, as well as a lifetime of habits and connections, and moving itself is such a hassle. That may be changing as Americans in general become more mobile and less tied to place. Families (including our own!) have become so spread out that it's hard to define where home is anymore; thanks to relatively cheap air travel, just about any family can get together for the holidays, so what does it matter where the grandparents live?

If you're considering a move, do your research carefully! Some states, like New Hampshire, appear to be bargains because they have no income or sales tax—until you look at the sky-high property tax rates, which vary by community. (According to the nonprofit Tax Foundation, New Hampshire has the second highest per-capita property tax rate in the nation, after New Jersey.) Some states have much higher health care costs than others. And unless you already live in expensive areas of California or the Northeast, those trendy sunbelt destinations might not seem like much of a deal.

If you like the amenities of a big city but can't handle the expense, consider moving to a small college town. You'll find plenty of restaurants, shops, culture, and intellectual stimulation for a lot less money. Not all college towns are cheap, but bargains can be found. For example, auto-industry woes have put a lid on real estate prices in Michigan, including Ann Arbor (home of the University of Michigan). Right now you can buy a nice Craftsman bungalow within walking distance of the campus for less than the cost of a small apartment in Chicago. Ann Arbor, famous among other things for its jazz scene, is close to Detroit's major airport and an easy drive to Great Lakes recreation sites. Some great Web sites with research tools and comparative city and state data include www.taxfoundation.org, www.retirementliving.com, and www.bestplaces.net.

4. Drive cheaper cars.

We wrote in Chapter Three about the high cost of car ownership—especially when it comes to new cars, which depreciate rapidly. Those expenses really take a bite out of your retirement income. And driving spiffy new cars makes even less sense when you're not commuting every day. In many cases, a retired or even semiretired couple can get by with just one car. Here's another money-saving transportation tip: consider walking or riding a bike, which is free and invigorating. They do it routinely in Europe. If you live in a town that's conducive to walking or biking, try it; you'll save some money and stay in shape!

5. Consider a reverse mortgage.

If ou are 62 or older, a reverse mortgage is a way to generate income from your property investment. You get a loan for the

double take

Reverse Mortgages

David: Reverse mortgages can be an effective tool for dealing with the financial pressures of retirement. You're taking an idle asset worth maybe $400,000 or $500,000 and using it to draw income without having to move. So you get to stay in the house you love, and generate enough income to afford it. The popularity of reverse mortgages is soaring. According to the U.S. Department of Housing and Urban Development, the number of people taking out reverse mortgages has more than quadrupled over the past five years.

Jonathan: The downside to a reverse mortgage is that it's essentially the opposite of an investment. Here you're taking your home investment, which is designed to grow in value, and eroding its net worth over time. When you and your spouse die, your heirs will have to pay off the loan—probably by selling the house—thus reducing their inheritance. If you decide a reverse mortgage is right for you, shop around as you would on any other loan by examining the APR on the Truth in Lending statement and comparing closing costs and other fees. These things can be expensive. Your financial advisor may illustrate that you could do better by selling your home, downsizing (or renting), and investing the difference in a conservative income portfolio. Remember, too, that you'll also have to submit your home to an inspection, and repair any major problems that turn up.

sale of your house, versus traditional mortgages where you get a loan for your purchase. As a result, you can cash out your home's equity without having to sell. Here's how it works: you take out a mortgage on your home, but you don't make any payments until you die, at which point your house is sold to pay back the mortgage. (You could also pay back the loan before you die, if you decide to move.) The bank pays you in one of three ways: a lump-sum payment, monthly income, or a line of credit. Typically, a nonrecourse clause prevents the bank from tapping into any of your other assets should the home's value drop below the loan amount. It's even possible to get a reverse mortgage if you still owe money on your home; you can use some of the proceeds to pay off the old mortgage.

6. Consider an annuity—carefully!

An annuity is an investment contract with an insurance company, in which you make a lump-sum initial payment in return for either tax-deferred growth of the principal over time or monthly income, depending on the type of annuity. One chief advantage of annuities over mutual funds is that they provide downside protection; if you die, you can't lose any of your principal. In return, you'll be donating some of your growth, as well as steep fees, to the insurance company. Annuities can be extremely complicated, even if the underwriters make them seem simple. Always consult a financial planner who does not stand to benefit from the sale before buying an annuity.

David: The most popular annuities today are so-called income-for-life plans, which are designed to supplement your income rather than provide investment growth. There's a real appeal to receiving guaranteed monthly income for the rest of your life. But you will pay a lot for that guarantee—mostly in annual fees that can be double or triple the cost of mutual funds. Don't let anybody tell you that a 3 percent fee is not much money; over time in a large annuity, that could mean tens or even hundreds of thousands of dollars right out of your pocket! The peace-of-mind premium is expensive indeed.

Jonathan: Not only that, but when you do withdraw money from an annuity, it will be taxed at your income tax rate. By contrast, withdrawals from a mutual fund that are not part of a qualified retirement plan are taxed at the lower capital gains rate. Also, you should be aware that with income-for-life annuities, when you die the insurance company is off the hook; your heirs will get nothing at all. That's very different from traditional variable annuities that pay back your principal, plus any accrued interest, to your heirs. Again, you're paying dearly—or your heirs will pay, in the form of a reduced inheritance—for the security of an income for life.

David: In many cases you can do better on your own by putting your nest egg into a portfolio of mutual funds, then authorizing the fund to distribute a monthly income of 4, 5, or 6 percent of your previous year-end account value. As your account value grows, so will your monthly payments. Of course, if the account value drops, your income will take a hit—but at least you won't be cannibalizing your principal. In summary, mutual funds are probably a better place to park your money, but annuities can make sense for someone who wants the upside benefits of investing in the stock market, with protection from catastrophic declines.

Bottom line: Planning a late-stage life of meaning makes it easier to accept what happens, to be content with your situation, and to live longer. "Retirement has its daily challenges, just like the rest of life," says Steve. "I guess you could say I'm stumbling through it, and learning more every day. Both my parents made it to their nineties, so I hope to be learning for a long time to come."

Chapter Eight:

The Heart of the Matter: Finance for Couples

MONEY, MARRIAGE, AND TENSION

Meet John and Mary, a typical husband and wife. John works in a large downtown office building, where he talks on the phone a lot and goes to meetings. Mary works part-time in the billing department of a local medical group, then works full-time as a mother and housekeeper—raising their two children, doing the shopping, and running errands. At night, after helping the kids with homework and music practice, the couple has an hour or so to touch base before they collapse from exhaustion. Every few Saturdays, in between the soccer and hockey games, the fencing lessons, the piano recital, and the household repair projects, they get together and plow through the bills and credit card statements, trying to make sense of it all. It's tense:

usually the bills are overdue, and sometimes there is simply more month than money. They shuffle the bills and envelopes around silently, both of them clenching their teeth, afraid to say what's on their mind. Here's what they may be thinking:

John: I feel like I'm on this treadmill, and it keeps accelerating. Like I have to run faster and faster just to keep from falling off. The stress is awful. She just doesn't get it! I mean, does she realize how lucky she is to work part-time? As I see it, she leads a pretty nice life: a few hours' work three days a week, coffee with friends, a workout at the gym, a nice car . . . how hard can it be? And the spending is never-ending! Yeah, I know the kids and the house take a lot of work, but if she were just more organized, it wouldn't be such a big deal. I folded my own laundry in college. It takes, like, five minutes! She needs a plan, just like at the office. I'm working my butt off, making good money, and we have nothing to show for it! Sometimes I wonder if her job just increases our tax liability. If my dad knew that I need $4,000 a month just to pay our bills, he would absolutely freak! Something's gotta give.

Just once, I'd like to trade my job with hers, so she would know what I deal with. . . .

Mary: He's clueless. I know he's out there working hard, but I wish he would appreciate how hard it is for me, too. He thinks that my life is so much easier than his, but it's nonstop here. I'm up at six, making breakfast, packing lunches, coordinating school clothes, nagging to brush teeth, getting myself ready for work. After school it's driving to orthodontist appointments, carpooling to soccer, scheduling teacher conferences, getting the oil changed, taking Mom to the doctor, cleaning the house, spraying for ants, fixing the sprinkler, picking up *his* dry cleaning, scooping dog poop, cooking dinner, and folding laundry (which I doubt he's ever done in his whole life). When I worked full-time before the kids, I had my own money, and got more respect. Now I actually work harder, for less pay, and I feel like I have to beg for money just to pay for our lifestyle. I mean, it's not like I'm buying Prada bags; the kids outgrow their sneakers every few months! He goes to Home Depot for some nails and comes back with a table saw. Something's gotta give.

Just once, I'd like to trade my job with his, so he would know what I deal with. . . .

Money is not really the root of all evil, but it certainly contributes to a lot of marital stress. Poor communication about money is a recurring theme in troubled marriages. At best, arguments and misunderstandings over money cause hurt feelings. The financial stress is then self-fulfilling, because when couples no longer work and plan as a team, the money problems grow deeper. At worst, fighting over money is a principal cause of divorce; tragically, divorce itself then leads to even more economic hardship for both partners, who are now paying for separate homes, among other increased expenses.

It all seemed simpler for our parents' generation. Dad went to work, Mom stayed home, and no one ever talked about money—at least not in front of the kids—much less argued over it. Of course, it wasn't really so rosy; it just appears that way through the prism of our own experience.

Today's boomer families can be quite complicated. For starters, many of us have two-income households; how do we divide up the money and obligations? We might be starting second families after a divorce; it's common for a new spouse to resent supporting a partner's previous spouse and children, as often happens after alimony and child-support judgments. Then there are nontraditional families, like those carefree spirits who never got married but didn't let that stop them from raising children; what are their financial rights and obligations? Even traditionally married couples often live together before the wedding, establishing patterns of independent financial management that (for better or for worse) last for decades. Finally, gay couples, many with children, are trying to sort out finances in a legal climate that is changing rapidly.

Against this complex backdrop, paint in the myriad emotional responses that money triggers. On a purely academic level, money is simply a convenient way to trade labor. For example, it's obvious that a great deal of labor is required to make a car. You could try making one in your garage, but it would take you a very long time; it's more efficient for a large carmaker to mass-produce cars in a factory while you perform some *other* labor with your time. Trading your labor for the labor of the auto-plant worker is where money comes in.

That's the Economics 101 version of money. The *real-world* version is infinitely more complex. Money is about power, control, and personal identity. For many people, money is a major determinant of self-worth. It's no wonder we have disagreements about this subject!

This chapter will help you and your partner address your financial differences and work together toward common goals. The most important thing to know is that it's okay to feel differently about money—so long as you understand each other. Let's start with a test.

UNDERSTANDING YOUR MONEY DIFFERENCES

Answer the following questions, then see how your answers stack up to your partner's.

1. It's a busy Saturday night at a local restaurant, and the service at your table has been less than attentive. Your reaction is:

    A. Leave a small tip to reflect the level of service.

    B. Leave the standard 15 percent; the waitress is doing the best she can.

    C. Leave a generous 20 percent tip because you're

richer than the waitress and you like to "spread it around."

2. The Federal Trade Commission just approved your company's merger with the Global Empire Corporation. As part of the deal, your company is immediately vesting all matching contributions to employee retirement accounts, netting you $124,000 overnight. Your reaction is:

A. Let's buy a boat!

B. This is bad news! When companies merge, they often vest benefits to encourage early retirement and ease consolidation. If not enough employees take the bait, there could be layoffs. I better start looking for a new job.

c. This is good news! Our retirement account can use the boost—but we can probably afford a nice dinner out to celebrate.

3. In the largest stock sell-off in recent memory, the Dow plummets 12 percent in one day. Your reaction is:

A. I'm in the market for the long term and feel comfortable waiting this out.

B. I'm uncomfortable losing that much in one day and would feel better if more of my money were in safer investments.

C. What a great opportunity to buy Google cheap!

4. Your daughter just started high school, and it's clear you don't have much money saved for college. Your reaction is to:

    A. Make sacrifices to quickly boost your savings over the next four years so she can go to Yale.

    B. Explain to her that unless she gets scholarships and takes out loans, she will have to attend a public university.

    C. Encourage her to save her own money to help cover college costs.

5. Your spouse says that because he or she earns more than enough money to support the family, you can quit your job and be a full-time parent. You feel:

    A. Unappreciated. Your job may not pay as much, but contributing financially to the family is important to you.

    B. Relief! You hate your high-stress job, dread the long commute, and would derive more satisfaction and meaning from caring for your children.

    C. Conflicted. You have a strong parenting instinct and feel you should be raising children, but you also like working with adults and earning some money of your own.

And the correct responses are . . .

All of the above. There are no wrong answers (although we probably wouldn't advise many people to buy a boat with their retirement savings), just *different* answers. The point of this exercise is to put your differences about money on the table.

Look at it this way: when you and your spouse go to a restaurant, do you always order the same thing? Of course not. When you go to a movie, do you immediately agree on what to see? Fat chance! It's the same way with money. Each of us is "hardwired" to think about money in a certain way. Often our emotions about money are deeply rooted in our upbringing. If money was a source of tension in our family, that will affect how we think about it. If money was never discussed at home that, too, can have an impact on our adult life.

But just because we feel differently about money doesn't mean we can't succeed financially. The key is understanding where your spouse is coming from, and being sensitive to his or her point of view. For example, some people who grew up in a financially dysfunctional family may become irrationally conservative about money. Out of fear that the money will run out, such people can't bring themselves to buy anything—even necessary purchases within budget. Someone like that would not be pleasantly surprised by expensive gifts from a partner; in this case, diamonds would *not* be a girl's best friend. If you know that your spouse is uncomfortable spending money, you may want to be more vigilant about discussing major cash outlays in advance, giving your spouse ample opportunity to express concerns. You wouldn't raise your children without lots of planning and conversation; so, too, should a husband and wife have an honest and ongoing dialogue about their finances. Let's take a closer look at how couples can communicate effectively about money.

Meet Rob and Susan (not their real names, but they are very real people), a married couple in their thirties who live in the Midwest. Until recently, Susan, a mortgage broker, was the primary bread-winner in the family. Her income during the boom real estate years was enough to support the family while Rob continued his college studies. But with two small children at home and the real estate market slowing down, Susan figured it was a good time to scale her career down into a part-time job. Rob, meanwhile, finished school and started his own career, selling radio frequency identification (RFID) technology to large retail chains. Now the tables are turned, and Rob is earning most of the money.

The role changes could have been difficult for both of them, but fortunately Rob and Susan have an excellent attitude about sharing money that dates back to the beginning of their relation-ship. "I wish I could say we had planned it that way," says Rob. "What happened was, when we were starting out, Susan worked at a bank and got free checking. So naturally we figured we'd save a little by keeping all our money in her checking account. We weren't thinking about the future implications of having a joint checking account, but now I can see how that decision put us on a track of transparency about money."

As a result, says Susan, their career shifts have been relatively seamless—even though with Susan down to two work days a week, they are earning less money these days. "We definitely have to rein in our spending a bit," she says, noting that some home improvement plans are on hold. "But when we do spend money, we make sure we're in agreement. It's not 'his money' and 'her money.' It's *our* money."

THE PATH TO JOINT PLANNING

To get couples talking about money, we follow a simple three-step process that we call Now, Then, and How. These steps, outlined below, will put you on a lifetime path of financial sharing that becomes habit-forming because it is goal-oriented.

1. Now
(Assessing where you are today)

This is where you, as a couple, sit down and take your financial snapshot—the basic budget-making exercise that we detailed in Chapter Three. Before you can plan for the future, you need to know where you stand right now. That means totaling up your assets (everything you own, including equity in your home and retirement accounts) and liabilities (everything you owe, including mortgage and credit cards). If you're young, chances are you owe more than you own when your mortgage is factored in. But if your annual debt payments including your mortgage are more than a third of your joint income, paying down loans should be a high priority; it's hard to save for future goals when all your disposable income is going to debt service.

It could be that you and your partner have some separate accounts, or maybe separate credit cards. There's nothing inherently wrong with that (see below), so long as you are both completely open and honest about it. *Hidden accounts and secret debts are not allowed!* Without complete trust, your financial partnership will never thrive.

When you're finished, your budget should give you a detailed picture of your monthly income and expenses. But you should go beyond the dollars and cents to share the things about your financial life that you're most proud of. For example, one source of pride could be hitting $100,000 in your 401(k). Then talk about the aspects of your financial picture that you are the least proud of. (Do we hear credit card debt?)

It's very important that you have this conversation—even if just one of you pays the bills, or earns the money, or typically "worries" about the budget. No, you can't get out of this exercise by saying, "My husband takes care of the money" or "That's my wife's department." *His and hers is for bathroom towels, not financial planning.* If, after making a plan, you want to divide up the day-to-day duties, no problem. But the planning must be done jointly. The reason is that people who help generate a plan have a sense of ownership and are much more likely to follow through. If, on the other hand, the plan is simply dictated to you by your partner, it will feel like a straightjacket, not a team effort. Naturally if your partner comes up with the plan alone, it will most likely reflect his or her priorities, not yours.

Some of you might be saying, "But I'm *terrible* at math! I don't have a clue how to balance a checkbook! I don't have time! I trust my husband! I let my wife figure that out!"

Look, you don't have to be Einstein to do this. It's not brain surgery; it's not even pulling teeth. It's a conversation that you need to have. If you hate adding and subtracting, go ahead and let your partner wield the pencil. But you need to be at the table, talking it through. Trust us—you'll be glad you took the time.

2. Then
(Defining your dreams for the future)

Here's where it gets interesting. It's time to put away the calculator and dream a little. Get specific: where do you see yourselves in two years? Five years? Ten years? What does retirement look like to you? Where would you live, if you could live anywhere? What's your ideal job? Do you dream of staying home with the kids, or going out and conquering the world? Talk about the details: what major expenses are coming up in the next year? (Perhaps a car.) How about the next three years, or ten? (Like a home renovation, or a daughter's wedding.) Be sure to plan for long-term expenses like your kids' education. Write it all down!

When Jonathan teaches seminars in financial literacy, he hands out a questionnaire:

The year is 2020. I am ____ years old. Our children are
____ years old. We are living _____. Our greatest

> accomplishment together has been _____. I have per-
> sonally accomplished my lifelong dream of _____.

Think of this as a letter to yourself. It forces you and your partner to think about where you envision yourselves in the future. It's possible that your dreams will differ, and they may well change over time. That's okay; you'll find that having an ongoing discussion encourages you to make room for each other. Keep talking. Couples often find after many years that the greatest accomplishment of their life was simply spending it together as best friends. We are not experts, but it seems like that kind of satisfaction, (which trumps any material gain), only comes from an open, honest relationship. Earlier we talked about how money is often a symbol for so many larger issues in life. Well, here's another way that money "talks": you could say that getting your financial house in order is just a warm-up for a lifetime of sharing.

3. How
(Calculating how you'll get there from here)

This is a hot button in many relationships: how to make the money work. It's a lot easier when you've done steps one and two, because by now you've got your goals in sight. But the details can trip up the best-laid plans. Here are questions we hear all the time:

- Both of us work, but he earns a lot more than I do; who pays for what?
- Who keeps track of the bills?
- Who manages the investments and decides how to allocate?
- Which of us should be saving in a 401(k)?
- How do we set spending limits for each other that preserve the budget but give us some independence?

In general, we recommend that married couples pool their resources into a joint account and simply pay all their bills out of it. It shouldn't matter who earns more or less; you're sharing everything! And just because a nurse earns less than a software marketing executive doesn't make her job any less important. (Many would argue the opposite.) Likewise, a stay-at-home dad works just as hard as a go-to-work mom, and vice versa. Our friends Rob and Susan have had joint accounts, and credit cards, for years.

The same goes for savings. Check out the chart on the following page to see how a monthly savings regimen can grow over time. Notice the ratio between contributions and earnings. Any savings not deducted from your payroll should come out of your joint account. And if both of you have jobs with 401(k) plans, both should be funded to the maximum. Self-employed people should fully fund their IRA, SEP, or Keogh plans; remember that nonworking spouses of qualifying workers are eligible for their own traditional and Roth IRAs.

None of this means you have to pool every penny. We think

every relationship should make room for individual needs; after all, you agreed to be joined in matrimony, not joined at the hip! Some couples like to keep separate checking accounts that are distinct from the joint bill-paying account. It's like a place to stash your allowance—but you don't have to call it that. It's your discretionary income. That way, you can each have your own debit card for your own account. (Some couples keep separate credit cards, which is okay only if you can pay off the balances every month—and provided both partners see the statements.)

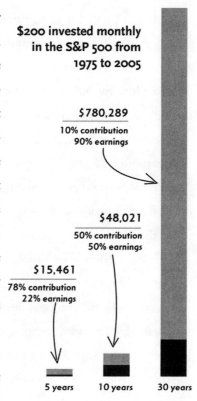

$200 invested monthly in the S&P 500 from 1975 to 2005

$780,289
10% contribution
90% earnings

$48,021
50% contribution
50% earnings

$15,461
78% contribution
22% earnings

5 years   10 years   30 years

Having your own bank card linked to a dedicated account is particularly helpful if one or both partners travel on business a lot. That way, when one partner withdraws the maximum on a certain day, the other partner isn't stuck with no way to get cash.

Even with separate discretionary accounts, a lot of couples have arguments over personal spending levels—variations on the "What's-in-the-Shopping-Bag Blues." One buys tools, the other buys shoes—and when the bills come due at the end of the month, surprise! The best way to avoid hard feelings over spending is by sticking to a careful budget that allows for discretionary purchases within bounds. If everybody plays by the same rules, no one is to blame.

Even Rob and Susan, who have a pretty good money relationship, admit that spending can push buttons. Says Rob: "Susan might say she wants to buy a new piece of furniture. So I'm thinking $800, but in her mind it's $3,000. She goes through the whole process, makes the decision, and then I see the price tag and go, 'Whoa!' Because I don't have any emotion or energy invested in it, it's easy for me to say, 'No, that's ridiculous, we're not spending $3,000.' But she's got all this time and effort in the process, so the money almost becomes secondary to her. It's so important to make sure you both have the same expectations by talking about it up front."

Here's another idea: come up with a set limit that neither of you can spend without the permission of the other. It could be $50, or $100, or $500, depending on your budget. This is a great way to keep each other informed about spending habits—especially in the cell phone age.

David: I tried calling from the home center recently, but my cell phone didn't work in there. It must be all the metal that those big box stores are made out of.

Jonathan: No, I think the stores jam cell phone signals deliberately, to keep guys from calling their wives and asking permission to buy a new saw.

David: Wow, interesting theory! I wonder if the ladies' clothing stores are onto that one.

Jonathan: Has your wife ever called you from one?

David: Hey, now that you mention it . . .

Conspiracy theories aside, the important thing is that you're in agreement about how much to spend and how much to save—which doesn't always mean doing the same thing with your money. You can apply the same principle to long-term investments. If your partner likes risk and you like to play it safe, there's nothing wrong with having different asset allocations in your individual 401(k) or IRA accounts. In fact, mixing an aggressive portfolio with a conservative portfolio could be a great way to mitigate risk while allowing each of you to invest at your own comfort level.

So much for the basics of joint finance. Now let's look at some special situations.

FINANCIAL SMARTS FOR OTHER RELATIONSHIPS

Second marriages

Some expenses are tricky to handle jointly. Often in second marriages, one or both partners have alimony or child support payments from an earlier marriage. When that happens, the other partner can resent contributing to a previous family. Often it's best to keep such payments separate from the overall budget. And this is one case where it might be advisable for a married couple to file separate tax returns, because courts base support judgments on your total household income. That means a judge can consider your own income when determining how much money your partner must give his or her previous spouse and children—even if you were just married. Indeed, ex-spouses often petition the court for higher support levels when their former partner marries someone with a substantial income. In some states, filing separate tax returns won't help you; even a spouse's individual return can be subpoenaed for consideration. Obviously, you should consult a tax advisor and attorney if any of these issues apply to you. Beyond the tax and legal considerations, it's important—as always—to have frank and open discussions about financial matters pertaining to previous marriages.

Unmarried couples

The Woodstock generation didn't turn out to be quite as radical as it seemed back in the sixties, but it definitely overturned conventional rules of courtship and marriage. Today it's common for couples to live together before marriage—or never get legally married at all. It might not make any difference between you and your partner, but from a financial perspective there's a lot to consider.

For starters, unmarried couples miss out on tax breaks because they cannot file jointly. That's just the beginning. It has been estimated that, in the United States, married couples enjoy approximately 1,400 benefits generally denied to unmarried couples! To name just a few: next-of-kin hospital visitation rights, family health care benefits, joint Social Security and veteran benefits, estate tax exemptions, family insurance rates, joint child adoption, crime-victim recovery benefits, and domestic protection orders. Those rights come with obligations, of course: married couples are responsible for each other's debts (at least in community property states). And if things don't work out, they can't simply walk away without settling many financial concerns. But even in divorce, the laws spell out rights and responsibilities that are left vague for unmarried couples.

Owning a home can be especially complicated for an unmarried couple. Unless it is owned under joint tenancy, one of you will have priority ownership should you separate; the other may have no legal recourse to get his or her money out of the deal. And even if the home is jointly held, a separation could force a fifty-fifty split, even if one partner owns the majority of the home.

In a legal marriage, if your spouse dies without leaving a will (it's called *intestate*) his or her estate will in most cases automatically pass to you, under a legal doctrine called right of survivorship. In a nontraditional union, your partner's estate likely will pass to other relatives—no matter how long you have been living together. The exception would be life insurance, savings, and retirement accounts that list you as the primary beneficiary. Such beneficiary designations always take precedence, even over wills.

Many unmarried couples assume they are covered under so-called common-law marriage rules. These ancient provisions recognize couples as legally married if they have lived together for a significant (though unspecified) period and share the same last name; they date back to agrarian times, when formal marriage was mainly for "titled" people. In fact, although it might make you feel warm and fuzzy to know you and your partner are married under common law, only a handful of states give any legal weight to such marriages. Common law or not, in most states you'll be out of the picture if your partner dies intestate.

Given all these legal ambiguities, we recommend unmarried couples draw up what's called a cohabitation agreement that clearly states your financial relationship—who owns what, and who gets what in the event of separation or death. An attorney (preferably an attorney for each of you) should help you do this. Keep in mind that this is basically a business contract (so-called family law doesn't generally apply if you're not married), so it needs to be worded properly or a judge could void the whole thing.

Gay couples

Gay couples face most of the same issues as unmarried heterosexual couples—but if anything it can be even harder for gay partners to sort out property and other rights. Of course, much depends on where you live: laws regarding gay couples are, quite literally, all over the map. Gay marriage has been codified under statute in Vermont, where so-called civil unions confer all state rights and responsibilities of heterosexual marriage on gay couples, although federal marriage benefits do not apply. Some other states, by contrast, have passed laws specifically banning homosexual marriage, while in still others judges have ruled against laws restricting marriage to heterosexual couples. Meanwhile, many states that stop well short of allowing gay marriage have passed laws specifically prohibiting discrimination based on sexual orientation. The issue is far from resolved. Wherever they live, we recommend that gay couples protect themselves with cohabitation agreements, especially if significant income or assets are involved.

PLANNING FOR THE UNPLANNED

Terrorist attacks, tidal waves, tornadoes, hurricanes, earthquakes, floods, and fires—recent cataclysmic events remind us all about the importance of preparedness. What would you do if you were separated from your family? What if your town lost running water and electricity for weeks? How would you get by if you suddenly could not access bank accounts? Sadly, for many residents of the Gulf Coast these unthinkable conditions have been all too real. Yet, even so, most people are unprepared for disaster. Surveys have shown that even many residents of the San Francisco Bay area are largely resigned to the prospect of a major earthquake, but have no real plan.

Most of us will be lucky enough to avoid major disasters, but death strikes every family at one time or another, and preparing for the loss of your partner is an important part of any financial plan.

In this section we'll discuss what every family needs to know *before* an emergency or loss. Nothing we say can alleviate the pain of a tragedy, but having your financial house in order can certainly help you cope, and could even make the rest of your life easier.

Stocking your emergency file

Every family should maintain a file of important documents and records that might be needed in an emergency. As we mentioned in Chapter Two, it's a good idea to keep originals of important documents in a bank safe deposit box. (Boxes cost just a few dollars a year, and are often free to good customers.) But remember that anything left with the bank will be unavailable after business hours. So we recommend you keep the following backup file in a safe place at home—preferably in a small fireproof safe or box, available at any hardware or discount store.

- A checkbook, which is more useful than bank cards during a power outage.

- Account numbers for all your bank and investment funds. (You should have the passwords memorized.)

- Account numbers of car, home, life, disability, and other insurance policies.

- Social Security numbers of everyone in your family, including children.

- Copies of important medical records including health care powers of attorney.

- Copies of your will and any other estate documents.

- An inventory of your home possessions, preferably on CD or videotape. (Definitely have one of these in your bank safe deposit box as well; digital media can be destroyed by heat, even in a fireproof home safe.)

- Enough cash to cover two weeks of emergency expenses like food and shelter.

- Employee benefit handbooks.

- Key contact information, including phone numbers, for your family doctor, insurance agent, accountant, lawyer, and financial advisor.

Life insurance

A lot of life insurance gets sold to people who don't really need it, including children. The bottom line is that life insurance is meant to replace, for a reasonable period of time, the income of someone who supports other people. That's it; end of story. It doesn't make up for the grief of someone's loss, or provide you with an investment portfolio, or get your widow a villa in the south of France. Simply put, if your untimely death would cause a financial hardship to dependents, you need life insurance. If you have no dependents, or if your assets are already large enough to support them, you don't need life insurance. Unless your child is a movie star who supports the family, she doesn't need life insurance.

Does that mean a stay-at-home parent needs no life insurance? Not at all! Consider what would happen if your stay-at-home spouse died suddenly. Who would care for your children and take care of the house while you go off to work? If the answer is, "I'd have to hire a nanny and a housekeeper," then your spouse needs life insurance, just like you do.

Now that we've narrowed down the field of life insurance candidates, two questions remain: What type of insurance, and how much?

David: There are two basic types of life insurance: term and whole-life. When you buy a term policy, the insurance company agrees to pay your beneficiaries a specific amount of money if you die anytime during the term—typically twenty years but as little as one or as many as thirty. A whole-life policy, on the other hand, insures you for the rest of your life, and you also earn a return on your premiums, which are invested.

For my money, term life insurance is the way to go. It's inexpensive, assuming you buy it before age fifty and have no health problems, and it gives your survivors exactly what they would need: a lump sum of cash to invest and live off. When the term expires, it's assumed that your children will be grown and your savings will be enough to support your spouse. In other words, at that point you will be *self-insured.*

By contrast, when you buy a whole-life policy you will be paying for insurance long into old age, when you probably don't need it. And the investment feature of whole-life is not such a great deal. The commissions and fees are high; you can usually do better by putting that money in a mutual fund.

Jonathan: I agree about term life. Make sure you get *level term,* which means the annual payments are the same, or level, across the entire term of the policy. Note also that you will usually have to pass a physical before buying term life insurance.

David: Which is another way of saying that people with serious illnesses are usually out of luck. Also, if you're thinking of changing policies, don't cancel your old one until you get a clean bill of health from your doctor. And be careful about changing in mid-term: the older you are, the more expensive life insurance gets.

Jonathan: The next question is how much life insurance you need. It's tough to generalize because each family's situation is different. You might have a lot of investments, so your survivors need very little extra cash; why pay for a lot of insurance you don't need? On the other hand, if your savings are low and your spouse has limited earnings potential, he or she would basically need to replace your income in order to maintain the same lifestyle.

One way to calculate insurance needs is by figuring how much the payoff would generate in annual income if your family invested the cash. Remember from our retirement calculations that a safe annual withdrawal rate is 4 to 6 percent of the principal, depending on market conditions. So if you had a $1 million policy, your survivors could safely withdraw $40,000 to $60,000 annually—theoretically forever, assuming historic market conditions. You can do your own math, using whatever amount of annual income your family needs to maintain its lifestyle—factoring in existing savings and your partner's own income potential.

David: Another way to look at life insurance benefits is to assume that your surviving partner would not need your support forever. Presumably at some point he or she would find the strength to move on—perhaps remarrying, or starting a new career. That's how Rob and Susan see it. Both have twenty-year term policies through their employers; his pays $1 million and hers is for $500,000. "If I died, Susan could pay off the house and be comfortable for a while," says Rob. "But she'd have to go back to full-time work in ten or fifteen years."

Jonathan: No matter how you calculate coverage, keep in mind that inflation will take a huge bite out of the benefit. If you die in the twentieth year of your policy, the coverage will be worth about half what it was originally—and that's assuming modest inflation rates!

David: That's why we said earlier that life insurance is unlikely to leave your family feeling wealthy, unless you have a huge policy. Think of it as backstop security in the event tragedy strikes. At the very least, it should be enough to keep survivors from worrying about bills for a few years, until they can heal and get back on their feet.

Jonathan: The good news about life insurance is that benefits are tax-free; your survivors get it all. But the bad news is that it can often take many months before they will see the cash—especially if the circumstances of death are unclear. (Suicide, for example, is generally not covered in the first few years of a policy.)

Advance directives

The sad spectacle of the Terri Schiavo case made it clear how important it is for each of us to make our medical wishes clear, and in writing, while we are able to do so. A casual conversation with your spouse is not good enough! The U.S. Supreme Court has ruled that every American has the right to terminate life-support systems and die with dignity—but the catch is that most states do not allow doctors or hospitals to disconnect systems without the permission of the patient, who is often unable to communicate. The solution is putting your particular wishes in an *advance directive*, which is a generic term for a group of legal documents that explain your medical preferences and, most importantly, give a person of your choice—typically a spouse or child—the power to carry out your wishes.

Advance directives generally consist of two parts: a living will and a durable power of attorney for health care. A living will states whether or not you wish to be kept alive using all extraordinary measures (it's entirely your choice), and usually includes language to the effect that you wish to be relieved of pain, even if such measures hasten your death. Other language details your wishes regarding everything from experimental treatments to organ donation.

A durable power of attorney is a document that appoints an agent to make decisions for you if you are incapacitated. (It is called "durable" because it remains in effect even if you are unconscious.) Presumably your agent will base decisions on the conditions of your living will, but—here's the tricky part—he or she is not obligated to do so, since so many life-threatening medical issues fall into gray areas. And once you are incapacitated, a doctor or hospital must legally follow the orders of your agent, within the bounds of medical ethics. *The durable power of attorney carries more legal weight than your living will.* That's why it is so important that your agent be someone you trust completely—literally with your life.

You can have a lawyer draw up advance directives for $100 or so, or you can download free legal forms for every state from an excellent Web site, www.compassionandchoices.org. In addition to documents that are legally binding in your state, the download contains a worksheet that walks you through the process and explains everything in plain English. Your signature on the directives needs to be witnessed. You should keep the original with your important documents and make sure a copy goes into your permanent medical file with your primary care physician.

Wills and trusts

Many people are uncomfortable even thinking about a will, much less actually writing one. The subject seems to trigger negative feelings of death—a subject most of us would rather avoid.

Having a will does not hasten your inevitable death, but it does clarify your last wishes—and not just for your loved ones. Many important decisions regarding your estate likely will be made by a probate judge, according to the terms of your will. So what happens if you die without a will? Let's take a look:

- Any insurance policies, annuities, and savings or mutual fund accounts will go to the beneficiary listed on the account. Beneficiary designations are legally binding—which means if the beneficiary on your life insurance is your ex-husband, he will get the money, no matter how much your current husband protests. That's why it is very important to update your beneficiary lists after major life changes.

- Assets held jointly with your spouse, such as a house, will be passed to your spouse. Assets in your name only will pass to your spouse and children. If they are not alive or cannot be found, your grandchildren are next in line, followed by parents and siblings. If no living relatives can be found, your assets will become the property of the state.

- If your death leaves minor children without a parent, a judge will determine guardianship. In fact, a judge will do this even if you have a will—but the difference is,

your will can state your preferences for guardianship,
such as a sibling, so the judge has something to go by.

Jonathan: Okay, you might be saying, that all sounds reasonable. Why bother with a will? But wait: what if you and your spouse were to die tragically at the same time? Would your children, or siblings, know how you wanted to divide up your estate? Besides the big items like a home and cars, who gets the heirlooms—furniture, jewelry, and so on? It's not so simple, even in a modest estate.

David: Nor is it fast! Depending on where you live, probate can take an eternity—and it's expensive. You could easily burn through tens of thousands of dollars in legal fees settling an estate. Often people have to sell homes they have inherited just to pay for probate.

Jonathan: It happens all the time. Probate is necessary because when someone dies, an impartial observer—namely a judge— has to make certain that the will is legitimate, and that the proper people get what's due them. After all, the person who signed the will is gone. It's also a chance for people who feel they've been wrongly excluded from a will to make their case.

David: Fortunately, your heirs can avoid probate hell if you plan ahead and put your major assets into a *revocable living trust.* By transferring your assets to a trust while you are still living, there is no probate when you die; the assets simply remain in the trust, which will have a designated beneficiary—like an insurance policy.

Jonathan: A lawyer can help you draw up a trust; the price depends on how many assets you have. The important point is to *fund* it—that means transferring all of your major assets into the name of the trust. In the case of property, you'll have to pay deed recording fees, because you are basically "selling" your home to the trust. Don't worry: your name will still be on the deed as trustee, so as a practical matter nothing changes hands. And, as the name suggests, you can change a revocable living trust at any time.

David: Once you have a trust, your will is essentially a backup document that covers all of your belongings not listed in the trust. And a will is always the place to detail your wishes for guardianship of children, as well as your funeral and burial preferences.

If all of this sounds morbid, it really isn't. In fact, estate planning is about life, not death. Most people feel a great sense of pride and satisfaction after making a will. Knowing that your partner will be able to carry on if you're gone can be liberating for both of you. And once you've made these basic plans, you can move on to what's really important: your life together.

Chapter Nine:

Kids and Money

$269,520 (WITHOUT COLLEGE)

A ccording to recent data from the U.S. Department of Agriculture, that's how much the average American family will spend to raise a child from birth through age seventeen (the survey involved quarterly visits and interviews with about 5,000 households). And the study didn't even include college costs or private school education! When you consider everything that goes into raising children—housing, food, transportation, clothes, health care, entertainment—it makes sense. Our kids owe us an ice cream . . . a really big one (or maybe you'd better make that a martini).

Having kids not only changes our lives on an emotional level—some of us might even admit it matures us—but on a logistical and financial level as well. The financial side of raising your kids, from allowances (do they work?) to paying for college to "boomerang" arrangements (the return of the college grad, living once again at home) is an ongoing and tremendously fulfilling challenge. How do you help your child develop a good work ethic? What's the proper approach to saving money? How can you teach them about responsible credit before they fall into debt? Is there a way to inspire our kids to help those less fortunate? What about all the various college funding options, including 529 plans, the Coverdell IRA, UTMA accounts, and financial aid? We'll cover all of that in this chapter. Before we get into strategies, however, it's important to think about today's child-rearing environment—and how much it has changed since we were young.

DIFFERENT ERAS, DIFFERENT EXPECTATIONS

Parents in the 1940s and 1950s worked hard to skimp, save, and send their kids (today's baby boomers) to college. They had first-hand memories of the Great Depression. Our dad's mother (we called her Mimi), who was born in 1905, had countless stories about how families struggled through the Depression in Beaver, Pennsylvania. She remembered how neighbors would get together for potluck dinners in order to save on food. She told us how common it was to hear a knock on the back screen door and find a complete stranger standing there, hat in hand, hoping to clean gutters or rake leaves to make enough money to feed his family that night. We learned about the woman who had to sell her diamond engagement ring, and the family doctor in town who was occasionally paid in eggs or a can of ham. "Your grandfather was very fortunate," she would tell us. "He had work two days a week." Grandma Mimi didn't have to remind us how much more fortunate *we* were.

Today's kids need to hear these stories. We found a powerful collection of Depression-era photographs on the Web. It begins with a photo of the floor of the New York Stock Exchange on October 29, 1929, the day the market crashed. On that day, $30 billion vanished, banks failed (wiping out peoples' savings), and families were turned upside down. Check out the photos at www.english.uiuc.edu/maps/depression/photoessay.htm, and share them with your children.

Understandably, because of the Depression and World War II, America's next generation of parents was determined to offer only the best to their children. Incomes soared during the prosperous 1950s. Many older Americans that we interviewed suggest that we now have an entire generation of Americans with a much larger sense of entitlement. They may have a point. Here are a few examples of how things have changed:

	Kids then	Kids now
Sports:	Little League	$1,000 travel team
Transportation:	Roadmaster bike	Mom's SUV
Leisure activity:	Yahtzee	Xbox
Communication :	Yelling	Text messaging
Clothes:	Levi's	$100 designer jeans
Beverage:	Mom's lemonade	Starbucks
Acne cure:	Clearasil	Dermatologist

As parents, it's hard not to look back at the 1950s and 1960s—when we grew up—without being a little nostalgic. Today's environment feels so much busier, and so much more expensive! Paradoxically, while trying to provide the best for our children, we may be denying them some of life's most valuable lessons about dealing with failure, surmounting obstacles, delaying gratification—and of course, how to budget, live within our means, and save. In previous chapters we uncovered ways to get organized, save more, and invest wisely. Now, let's focus on effective ways to tackle two of our favorite subjects at once: kids and money.

Ages two to six

Families can start teaching children about the importance of work as early as age two by including them in your household chores. Even if a small child is simply watching you fold laundry, cut the grass, or load the dishwasher, he's observing you work. Consider that for children, playtime is their form of work—it's how they learn about the world. If they see you enjoying your own chores around the house, they'll get the message that adult work, like their own play, is not to be shunned but enjoyed and accepted as an essential part of life.

Get your toddler a piggy bank, preferably one that's see-through. (David's family still uses a five-gallon water cooler bottle to deposit the day's loose change). A young person may not know about passbook savings accounts, but she'll have fun watching the bottle fill up with coins over time. As they turn five or six, children can become involved in helping around the house. Paying them a modest amount when they contribute is a great way to include them in the family team, and begin motivating them to work and save.

Note that this strategy is different from paying an "allowance" every week. In our opinion, you should scratch the allowance and pay for each chore performed, which is more like the real world. Chores are a great way to build responsibility, relationships, and self-respect. A few times a year, it's fun for kids to "borrow" a few coins from their piggy bank and purchase a little toy or candy bar. Help them keep track of what it costs, though ("two quarters, one dime, and two pennies," you say, as you lay out the coins on the register counter). As you leave with your grinning tot, happily clutching her watermelon-flavored, ten-foot rope gum, remind her that she'll want to pay Piggy back: "We want Piggy's belly to keep getting fatter!" In the next day or two, help your child redeposit another sixty-two cents that she earned in the piggy bank. You've now shown her that stuff costs money, that you can save it, borrow it, and pay yourself back. And importantly, you made it fun! (Grandparents are often great at this.)

Age-appropriate chores for two- to six-year-olds include:
- Making the bed.
- Carrying dirty clothes to the laundry basket.
- Helping pick up the family room and bedroom.
- Bringing in the newspaper.
- Helping to feed the dog and cat.
- Setting napkins and spoons on the dinner table.
- Dusting.

Twins' tip: Don't be afraid to say no to purchases for your children. Kids today are experts at pushing our buttons to get what they want, but if they're given everything, they may never gain an appreciation for working hard to achieve a reward. At the very least, make an effort to go "halfsies" on purchases; often, kids who are forced to spend their own hard-earned cash will think twice about what they really want. You don't do your children any favors by constantly giving them money.

Ages seven to eleven

At this age, a more formal work/chore program can be implemented around the house. Unloading the dishwasher, setting the table, folding laundry, and taking the garbage out can all serve as opportunities to compensate children for their efforts.

Kids in their preteen years will be more influenced by their peers. They'll start tuning into what others are wearing, and may be more vocal about wanting these items. This is a perfect time to begin teaching about delayed gratification: that we can't always get what we want . . . at least not right away. Open up a savings account for them, preferably one they can track online. Some parents match their child's savings. Others will contribute a special "bonus" when savings thresholds are met—Johnny surpasses $100 in his savings account, and Mom and Dad contribute another $10 or $20 . . . now you're building a savings ethic! As they identify something that they want, encourage your children to write it down, or even clip out the picture in the magazine or catalog. This will help to motivate them further.

Age-appropriate jobs for seven- to eleven-year-olds include:
- Taking care of pets, including walking dogs.
- Cooking.
- Raking leaves, shoveling snow, cutting the grass.
- Cleaning more of the house.

- Helping do laundry.
- Loading the dishwasher.
- Playing with younger siblings.
- Organizing bake sales, lemonade stands, garage sales.

Twins' tip: Keep the money in the family. If you're busy, chances are you're paying other people to do things that you and a young helper could do together. Yard work, babysitting, shirt pressing— why not pay someone in your own family to do these jobs? Kids are more apt to help if you play their favorite music while working.

Ages twelve to sixteen

Beginning around age twelve, children can start focusing on additional ways to work outside the home and to build up their savings. As they earn money, come up with a percentage together for mandatory savings: 50 percent of their total earnings would be ideal, but anything over 30 percent will bulge the bank account. At this age, kids can be creative as they think about a summer job. Try to find something that's fun and different. Detailing cars, running a craft camp for neighborhood kids, and fixing computers are all possibilities. Jonathan's son opened a light bulb business, and sold bulbs to neighbors.

Young teens should also be encouraged to volunteer and give

to charities. There are dozens of options, through religious organizations, Scouting, and communities, for your teen to give either time or money to a worthy cause. It's best to start out slowly with something they really enjoy; a child who loves to read could help out shelving books at the library. You don't want this to be another "chore."

Lastly, if your child has not worked for adults outside the family yet, now would be a good time to start. By working for others, young people learn more about accountability and consequences. It's one thing when Mom and Dad lecture about "measuring twice." When kids hear the same lesson from another adult, they tend to listen more closely.

Traditional jobs for young teenagers:
- Babysitting.
- Landscaping, yard work.
- Car washing.
- Pet care.
- Newspaper route.

As your child moves into the workforce, be aware that federal and state child labor laws restrict many types of employment. On the federal level, kids under fourteen cannot be employed in any formal manner, except in newspaper delivery, acting, and certain farm labor. Kids under sixteen can only work limited hours during the school year. And some jobs, *including all forms of driving*, are not allowed for anyone under eighteen. Your state may well have even stricter laws.

Late teens to early twenties

As children enter high school, parents gain a wonderful opportunity to teach them about banking and investing. By opening a checking account and an investment account, your child can learn responsible money management while you're still available to supervise. These days, college students are easy prey for credit card companies, which routinely set up shop at freshman orientation and offer free T-shirts and 0 percent interest—for the first month. Before you know it, your student has overwhelming debts and skyrocketing interest payments that can last into adulthood. Today's average college grad already owes almost $30,000 in student loans. On top of that, almost 52 percent of young adults age eighteen to twenty-four also carry plastic. Their average monthly balance is $584 per card, according to myvesta.org, a nonprofit financial crisis center.

By helping your teen learn how to balance a checkbook, pay bills, and live within his means, you can head off a lot of trouble. Explain to your child that making minimum payments on a $2,000 credit card balance will mean spending more than sixteen *years* to pay it off (assuming no new charges are made!), racking up over $2,500 in interest fees. If your child has bank and credit card accounts, order a copy of her credit report and review it together. Finally, mutual

Double Take: The Work Ethic

David: Don't be shy about encouraging your child to get a very basic, minimum-wage job, especially if you live in a middle- or upper-class community. In many ways, the more they sweat the better. Your local restaurants, will almost always need dishwashers. (Your state could place age limits on employees at restaurants where alcohol is served.) In addition to earning money the hard way, a blue-collar job teaches young people about getting along with all kinds of different people. Similarly, if you live in a lower-income community, don't think that your son won't be able to caddy at a nearby country club. He'll learn a lot about a different way of life. One of the best gifts our parents ever gave us was the opportunity to meet (and work with) people from all walks of life.

Jonathan: I like the idea of down-and-dirty work for kids, up to a point. But I'm also in favor of kids getting more hands-on experience in fields that they truly love. Generally such work takes the form of unpaid summer internships, which can be arranged through a school guidance counselor. (To be legal, all unpaid work must be in an official work-study program leading to school credit.) All sorts of opportunities exist. We know a music-loving kid who got an internship helping out in a recording studio. Another kid interned as a cub reporter for a local paper, covering school issues. An outdoor enthusiast spent one summer working for his state's department of wildlife, helping to catch and count wild turkeys. Internships have a value far beyond money, and they should be a part of every kid's work experience.

funds are great for young investors to learn the basics of investing; many only require a $250 initial investment, with $25 minimums for additional deposits thereafter. Automatic investments can be set up directly from a checking or savings account.

Twins' tip: Don't forget start-ups! We all love hearing stories about multimillion-dollar businesses that started out as a zany idea in someone's garage. Encourage your kids to pursue their money-making interests. Even if an idea flops, the experience will be great—and young business ventures look impressive on a college application. A few ideas: setting up a landscaping company (our own high school business), music tutoring, pet care, and helping special-needs children.

Success Story: "I just did it, that's all . . . "

That's what David's neighbor Greg said when we asked him how he was able to accomplish so much at such a young age. Greg, eighteen, graduated from high school last year, and is a freshman at a large university in Michigan. For the past four years, he earned thousands of dollars each summer running his own landscaping business. Greg started in seventh grade, cutting grass for a handful of neighbors. Ultimately, he owned six mowers (two were the super-fast, self-propelled models with wide blades that you actually stand on), four gas-powered leaf blowers, and two power edgers. Last summer, Greg handled the weekly landscaping for twenty-five homes in the area. He had four guys working for him. He saved enough to buy his own truck, and, last October, Greg bought a house, fixed it up, and sold it for a small profit.

PAYING FOR COLLEGE

When we were sophomores at Dickinson College in 1981, the tuition was $5,840. Twenty-five years later, it has more than *quintupled*, to $31,800. If the tuition had simply matched overall inflation during that period, it would now cost just $12,517 for a year at Dickinson. In reality, tuition increased by more than two-and-a-half times the rate of inflation. Our alma mater is hardly alone; across America, college costs have skyrocketed over the last quarter century. Obviously, the increases cannot be pegged solely to the cost of running a school. The institutions don't always like to admit this, but supply and demand is the only rational explanation. We live in an age when college has become virtually mandatory, even for those with middle-class aspirations. If Johnny's parents will pay anything to get him into such-and-such college, naturally the college will be inclined to charge, well . . . anything! As long as parents and students are willing to pay through the nose (and borrow up to their eyeballs), college costs will continue to increase.

If you are already making sacrifices to get your kids through college, you'll appreciate the story of Sandy and Carl. Sandy, fifty-five, works for the federal government in Maryland. As a federal employee, she enjoys a benefit that our parents took for granted but that is increasingly rare for baby boomers: a guaranteed pension. When Sandy retires in a few years, she'll receive 80 percent of her salary for the rest of her life. Her husband Carl, sixty-five, recently retired from the same government agency and is receiving his own pension. It sounds like the makings of a comfy retirement—and, the truth is, Sandy and Carl are not too worried about their senior years. But the short-term picture is a lot more stressful. Sandy and Carl's twenty-one-year-old daughter is about to graduate from college, and their twenty-five-year-old son is finishing law school. In fact, the relatively low cost of public universities came as a relief to the couple, who put both kids through private school since kindergarten. Sandy estimates that, over the years, they have spent about $30,000 annually on education. To do that, they gave up nice vacations and stayed mortgaged to the hilt. "We don't want for anything, but we can't be extravagant," says Sandy. "If we could pay off our house, I'd feel more comfortable." She adds that her son, the new lawyer, already has a job that pays "way more than I make. I would hope he can help us in the future if we need it."

Like the stock market, the college market is often driven by emotion and perception. The long-term solution to runaway education bills will require change on every level of society—starting with our unrealistic expectations for higher education, and including a renewed commitment on the part of public universities to serve their local communities. In the meantime, state and federal legislators have created a kaleidoscope of tax-favored savings plans, grants, scholarships, credits, and loans to ease the sting. It's a typical American do-it-yourself environment—which is to say, there are a lot of choices that can be both liberating and overwhelming. Here's our take on the myriad ways to fund college.

Savings plans

Many parents worry that if they save too much for college, their child will be ineligible for financial aid. Here's the truth: if you are extremely wealthy, you will have to pay full freight, unless your child earns merit-based scholarships. If you are anything else, you will probably be eligible for financial aid. According to CNN Money, half of all families earning more than $80,000 qualified for financial aid in 2004. By law, federal aid (which constitutes the vast majority of funds available) assumes parents will make available 5.65 percent of their assets, not including retirement funds or home equity. (Some private schools expect you to contribute more, and may consider your home equity as well—another way of saying you could be asked to take out a second mortgage.) Students, on the other hand, are required to contribute much more of their own assets—at least 35 percent. So *where* you save can be just as important as how much; below, we'll explain how each savings plan gets counted toward financial aid. In any event, be aware that while saving less for college might increase financial aid, it could also leave your child saddled with student loans for years to come.

UGMA and UTMA custodial accounts

The acronyms refer to even more unwieldy titles: the Uniform Gifts to Minors Act and the Uniform Transfers to Minors Act. In both cases, these are ways to encourage tax-advantaged gifts to children. Parents, grandparents, or anyone else can set up an UGMA or UTMA account in a child's name at a financial institution and use the money to invest in almost anything, from stocks to annuities. Provided the child is age thirteen or younger, the first $800 of investment income is tax-free, the next $800 is taxed at the child's rate, and any additional income is taxed at the parents' rate. Once the child turns fourteen, all the income is taxed at the child's rate.

David: Since most fourteen-year-olds are assumed to be in the lowest tax bracket, the tax savings is significant. And don't forget that contributions to the account (up to $12,000 annually) are exempt from the gift tax. But there's one major catch: when the child becomes of legal age (as early as eighteen in some states), parents must cede control of the money to the child. And the kid can use it for anything he wants—maybe college, maybe snowboarding in Utah.

Jonathan: It's a little scary to think about. If that concerns you, consider an UTMA over an UGMA. While the two plans are basically the same, an UTMA gives parents control of the money for a little longer—possibly until age twenty-five, depending on the state. There is one other disadvantage to these accounts: they count as a child's asset, meaning 35 percent of the total must be factored into federal financial aid equations.

Coverdell Education Savings Accounts (CESAs)

Formerly known as Education IRAs, these new, improved accounts currently have a $2,000 annual contribution limit. Most brokerage and fund companies offer them. To qualify, your adjusted gross income must be less than $110,000 for a single filer or $220,000 for a married couple filing jointly. As with a Roth IRA, you get no tax break on deposits, but earnings are tax-free as long as they are used for qualified education expenses, which can include elementary and high school costs. (Note that, unlike a Roth, with a CESA you can't withdraw the principal penalty-free at any time.)

Jonathan: The nice thing is, you don't have to be working (or married to a working person) to open a Coverdell account—another way these plans differ from regular and Roth IRAs. That means even retired people can set up Coverdells for their grandchildren.

David: The money has to be drawn down by the time the child turns thirty, or it can be rolled over into a Coverdell for

	529 College Savings Plan	Coverdell Education Savings Account (ESA)	UGMA/UTMA Account
What you can do	Invest tax-free for college*	Invest up to $2,000 tax-free for any education level	Invest on behalf of a minor for any purpose
Ability to change beneficiaries	Yes	Yes	No
Controlled by	Person establishing the account	Person establishing the account	Custodian, until child is of age
Uses	Qualified college expenses	Primary, secondary, or higher education	Any expense that benefits the child
Impact on federal financial aid eligibility	Considered asset of parent or other account owner**	Considered asset of parent, if account owner**	Considered asset of child
Contributions state tax-deductible	Varies by state	No	No
State tax on earnings	Varies by state	Varies by state	Depends on child's age
Federal tax on earnings	No*	No, if used for qualified expenses	Depends on child's age
Penalties for nonqualified withdrawals	Federal income tax plus 10% penalty tax; state penalties vary	Federal income tax plus 10% penalty tax; state penalties vary	No
Contribution maximum per beneficiary	$200,000 to $300,000, depending on state	$2,000 per year	None
Investment options	Portfolios consisting of a variety of securities	Any non-insurance securities	UGMA: mutual funds, securities UTMA: mutual funds, securities, real estate, royalties, patents, and paintings
Estate-planning impact	Contributions are removed from estate***	Contributions are immediately removed from estate	Contributions are immediately removed from estate
Income limitations	No	Yes	No

another child. Otherwise you'll pay a 10 percent penalty as well as taxes. If your child dies or is disabled, the penalty is waived.

Jonathan: Coverdells are considered parents' assets, which mean that 5.65 percent of the total is factored into federal financial aid calculations. That's better than a UGMA or UTMA, but still something to consider.

Prepaid tuition plans

In these state-sponsored plans, you buy future college credits at today's cost. If tuition goes up (a good bet), you're locked in at the current rate—quite a deal if your kid is currently five years old! Plans differ from state to state so it's hard to generalize, but most require that you start the contract before the child reaches a certain

Notes for College Funding Table on opposite page:

*Withdrawals from 529 plans made after December 31, 2010, will be federally taxable unless the law allowing the federal income tax exemption is extended. Earnings on nonqualified withdrawals may be subject to federal income tax and a 10% federal penalty tax, as well as state and local income taxes. The availability of tax or other benefits may be contingent on meeting other requirements.

**Distributions for qualified educational expenses are not counted as parent or student income in the determination of federal financial aid eligibility.

***If you choose to take advantage of the accelerated gift tax benefit and you die within 5 years, a prorated portion of the contribution will be subject to estate tax. If you contribute more than $12,000 in a particular year, you must file IRS Form 709 by April 15 of the following year. For more information, consult your tax advisor or estate planning attorney.

age. The money gets invested, and the earnings (which will go to the school) are exempt from federal and, in most cases, state income tax. Any adult can take out a prepaid tuition contract in a child's name. If your child gets scholarship money (or dies or is disabled), you'll get your money and investment return back.

Jonathan: I like the fact that contributions to these plans qualify as exemptions to the gift-tax up to the maximum allowable $12,000 per year—and because of a five-year averaging provision, you can sock away $60,000 in one year, gift-tax free. But the downside is that you're locked into your kid attending a public school in the state where you took out the contract. If your son gets into Harvard or decides to follow his girlfriend to the University of Hawaii, you'll only get back a portion of your money.

David: Another problem is that the plans only cover tuition, not all the other college expenses. And you might earn more money by investing on your own; it all depends on how much tuition costs continue to rise. There are a lot of unknowns here.

529 college savings plans

Like prepaid tuition plans, 529s are state-sponsored, but they are much more flexible. Instead of buying tuition credits, your contributions are simply invested in either preset portfolios (geared to the child's age and time to college enrollment), or mutual funds that you select. Funds in a 529 plan can be used at accredited public or private schools nationwide (and some foreign schools), not just in the plan's sponsor state. Contributions above $12,000 are subject to gift tax, but withdrawals are exempt from federal taxes if used for qualified college expenses. Contributions may also be state income tax-deductible, depending on the plan.

David: The great thing about 529s is that contribution limits are high, with plan maximums from $100,000 to more than $300,000, depending on the state. And as with prepaid tuition plans, you can avoid the gift tax for up to $60,000 in contributions for one year, using five-year averaging. These are great college savings vehicles for people who have just inherited money or who otherwise have a lot of cash to sock away right now for college.

Jonathan: I agree. But one catch with 529s is that your investment options are somewhat limited, and you're at the mercy of the plan's financial manager. That doesn't mean you have no choice: because 529s are good in any state, you don't have to

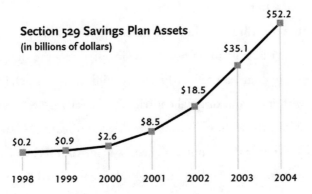

Section 529 Savings Plan Assets
(in billions of dollars)

$52.2
$35.1
$18.5
$8.5
$2.6
$0.9
$0.2

1998 1999 2000 2001 2002 2003 2004

Source: Investment Company Institute and College Savings Plans Network

invest in your own state's plan; you can shop around to find a plan with the best return on investment, or a higher contribution limit. In addition, you're allowed to change, or roll over, your 529 once a year. When shopping around, don't just look at how a plan did last year. Pay attention to its five-year performance. A great Web site comparing 529 plans is www.savingforcollege.com.

David: But keep in mind that you won't get the state income tax deduction if you buy into an out-of-state plan. Also, under federal financial aid rules, a 529 is the parents' asset.

Regular investment and retirement accounts

You can also set up a regular investment account earmarked for your child's education. Investment choices are unlimited, and if the money isn't used for college, it simply increases your retirement funds.

David: In particular, a Roth IRA is great way to save for college because contribution limits are much higher than for Coverdells. You won't be able to withdraw the invested income (unless you happen to be at least $59^1/_2$ when your child starts college), but you *can* withdraw your original contributions at any time. Over years of saving, those contributions can be significant. Meanwhile, you'll still have the earnings socked away for your retirement.

Jonathan: Best of all, because a Roth is considered a retirement account, none of the money counts toward financial aid.

Special tax credits and deductions

Don't forget that the IRS allows a tax deduction of up to $4,000 annually for college expenses. The deduction applies only to tuition and other costs related directly to education—not room and board, sports, medical insurance, and so on—and the student or students must either be yourself, your spouse, or your dependent. Your modified adjusted gross income cannot exceed $160,000 (married filing jointly) or $80,000 (single). Funds from tax-free accounts like Coverdells can't count toward the deduction, but student loan money can. Gifts from other people, like grandparents, cannot be deducted—from either your taxes or their own.

Even better in most cases are two tax credits. The *Hope Scholarship Credit* provides up to a $1,500 tax credit per year for the first two years that a dependent in your family attends college in a degree program. Keep in mind that a *credit* is much better than a *deduction* because it gets subtracted directly from your tax bill! To qualify for the Hope, you must incur tuition or other qualified expenses (again, room and board don't count) totaling at least $1,500 per year for each student. The payments cannot come from tax-free investment plans. To get the full credit, your modified adjusted gross income currently needs to be less than $87,000 (married, filing jointly) or $43,000 (single). The credit is gradually reduced until your modified adjusted gross income reaches

$107,000 (married, filing jointly) or $53,000 (single), at which point it is phased out. There are no limits to the number of credits you can claim in any year—so if you have triplets in college (it happens!), you can deduct $4,500 from your tax bill. You can't claim the Hope credit and the above mentioned tax deduction in the same year, however. But if your income qualifies you for the Hope, it's usually the better deal.

The second tax credit is the *Lifetime Learning Credit.* This one has the same basic restrictions and qualifications as the Hope, but it's good for up to $2,000 per year, per family (triplets don't get a break this time), and you can claim it for every year in which you are supporting a student in your family. (Unlike the Hope Scholarship, with the Lifetime Learning Credit the student does not have to be enrolled in a degree program.) You can't claim the Lifetime Learning Credit and the Hope Credit for the same student in the same year; if you have only one student in college, the Lifetime is the better way to go.

Student loans

According to the Student Loan Marketing Association (Sallie Mae), since 1966 more than 40 million students and their families have borrowed more than $270 billion in federal student loans to pursue higher education. In 2005, the average debt upon graduation was a whopping $27,600—more than triple what it was a decade earlier. The Department of Education estimates that 39 percent of graduates have unmanageable student loan debt—not surprising, given that since 2000, wages for recent college graduates have actually *dropped* while rent and other living costs have shot up considerably.

Time was when the biggest hurdle after graduation was finding a job. Now it's paying off the loans. It's often said that student loan debt is considered "good" because it's an investment in your future. But that's true only to a point. Too much college debt will be a major drag on your child's lifestyle, no matter what kind of job she lands with her new degree. It could even hamper her ability to follow her dreams. Suppose your daughter graduates from law school with the goal of working in advocacy—helping disadvantaged inner-city families with housing complaints, or representing battered women. Well, if she owes $80,000 in student loans (the national average for law grads), she probably can't afford to represent poor people; she'll need to take a corporate job. Maybe someday she'll return to her dream, maybe not. You can see how debt can drive career decisions.

If you or your child must borrow money for college, here's a good rule of thumb: Estimate how much money the borrower is likely to earn immediately after graduation. Student loan payments should total no more than 10 percent of that income.

While we're on the subject of loans, the federal government is now offering college loans to parents. They're called Parent Loans for Undergraduate Students (PLUS), and they allow you to borrow the entire cost of college (less financial aid). The loans are not collateralized, and you can pay them back over ten years. There is no needs test, but you must demonstrate good credit. Right now, PLUS loans have a variable interest rate capped at 9 percent, but a law change is expected to usher in fixed rates.

Financial aid

As we mentioned, most financial aid comes from the federal government, in the form of grants, scholarships, and work-study programs. In addition, schools, states, local communities, and private organizations offer many forms of need- and merit-based aid. When Jonathan worked in admissions at Dickinson College, there was a "Great Wall" between financial aid and admissions. Unfortunately, the high cost of college has forced most schools to consider ability to pay when deciding whether or not to accept a student. So it is very important to investigate aid options before applying to schools. Start with the U.S. Department of Education's Web site, www.ed.gov. Also check out www.fastweb.com to search for scholarships. And your child's high school guidance counselor should know about local scholarships.

Rick Heckman, senior associate director of financial aid at Dickinson, advises parents to leave no stone unturned: "Check with your employer, your church—any organization you belong to that might offer scholarships." Rick advises families of limited means to apply for full financial aid at every college their child is applying to. "That may mean filling out multiple applications," he says, "starting with the FAFSA [Free Application for Federal Student Aid] and the CSS financial aid profile from the College Scholarship Service—the same people who do the SAT tests. Some schools also have their own applications. Deadlines are all over the map, so you need to research carefully."

Rick says it's wise to have some lower-cost state schools as a backup, in case the aid you're hoping for doesn't come through. And he offers some advice for students hoping to get merit-based financial aid: "Get good grades! A 4.0 high school average goes a long way. We also like to see students who have clearly not just taken the easy courses, but who have applied themselves in challenging ways."

Rick says a lot of ambitious kids load up on extracurricular activities to impress aid officers, but sometimes it backfires. "I like a student who distinguishes herself, not necessarily in dozens of activities, but by meaningful participation in a couple of activities that really demonstrate leadership and commitment." So there you have it from the expert. Now sharpen those pencils and get to work!

Of course, before you get to spend your money on college, your kid has to get in. We can't leave the subject of college without a few words from our own admissions expert.

AN INSIDE LOOK AT
GETTING INTO COLLEGE

As the former assistant director of admissions at Dickinson—a highly selective liberal arts college—Jonathan knows what really counts when it comes to getting in. Some of it is common sense; some of it isn't very intuitive at all. Here's the view from the other side of the desk:

1. An interview <u>can</u> make a difference.

Most colleges and universities will tell you that having your child interview doesn't affect the admissions decision. Don't believe it! Especially if your child is "on the cusp," a glowing interview can make all the difference. Many admissions officers take notes from the interview, and include them in the student's file. I personally have accepted hundreds of students based upon the interview. Students, here's how to ace that interview:

- **Tell your parents to keep quiet.** Admissions officers don't care about parents. They want to get to know *you*.

- **Show enthusiasm!** During admissions season, I'd have to complete seven or eight forty-five-minute interviews every day. Believe me, that time can feel like an eternity with a monosyllabic responder.

- **Ask great questions.** That does not include, "What's your student-teacher ratio?" If your question can be answered in the college catalog, don't ask it. Use the interview to gain personal insight from the dean. "Do you ever go to student art shows?" would be a great question.

- **Meet your teachers.** If you love Japanese, meet with someone in the Japanese department. If you're a good lacrosse player, make sure you see the coach. Professors and coaches can have a lot of pull in the admissions process, and they are eager to get interested students in their departments.

- **Don't overdo it.** You don't need to bring your hundred-page art portfolio, or your dance tapes from the sixth grade. A simple letter of recommendation from a trusted source, or a game tape, can suffice.

- **If the school is your first choice, tell them!**

2. Focus on your transcript, not your test scores.

Most admissions officers will tell you that the best predictor of a student's ability is course work. Many colleges are even making the SAT optional. So take challenging courses, and do well in them. If your school does not weight advanced placement or honors level classes, make sure to tell the admissions office. I always preferred to see a B in an AP course than an A in a regular one.

3. Apply for early decision!

If you know that a school is your top choice, apply early. Here's why: colleges and universities pay close attention to their *yield*, which is the percentage of accepted students that actually enroll. If a college has a yield of 33 percent, it needs to make three "admit" decisions for every student expected to enroll. All those admissions make the school look less selective in guide-books. When a student applies for early decision, the school *knows* that student will enroll, which saves them having to make two additional acceptances. Make it easy for them to admit you by applying early.

4. Demonstrate leadership.

It doesn't matter in what area—Scouting, sailing, fencing, church—college admissions people want to see a passion for something. Their job is to put together a well-rounded, diverse class of freshmen with a variety of interests and backgrounds. We used to call it "the hook." You'll go far if you have something that sets you apart from the crowd.

TWINS' TIP FOR COLLEGE SENIORS: LANDING YOUR FIRST "REAL" JOB

How impressive can anyone's résumé be at age twenty-one? Most of us didn't have a whole lot to point to when it came to work experience. If your college senior is looking for a job, try what David did back in 1984:

> *In March of my senior year, I got a list of Dickinson College alumni in the Philadelphia area. I started making phone calls, explaining that for the next few months, I wanted to gather information about a wide variety of marketing careers. I said I wasn't looking for a job—or even a job interview—until later that year, which*

removed some of the pressure on both sides. Instead, I said, "I'll be in town on March 19th and 20th, and I'd love to stop in for five minutes and learn about what you do for a living." At this point, most of the people I talked to were very pleasant, and agreed to see me. Some, of course, said that they were too busy, which was fine. At the meeting, I'd find out a lot about them: what was your major at college? Did it help you to get this position? (Most said no.) How did Dickinson prepare you for this career? How do you enjoy your job? What's the most challenging aspect of being in marketing? And so on.

Five minutes later, I would thank them for their time, shake hands, and leave. I did this with about a dozen alumni, following up with thank-you notes to all, handwritten on the college's stationery.

Five or six weeks later, I repeated the process—only this time, the questions were much more specific: "I noticed in last year's annual report that your division's revenue took a 20 percent hit in the fourth quarter. Did it have anything to do with your competition's new product launch that fall?" Or: "Covering five states the way you do must be tough, especially considering your sales growth over the last six months; how do you determine when it's financially viable to bring on another salesperson?"

At that point, some of my "targets" started taking an interest in me! They'd fumble around for my résumé (which I left with them the last visit) and say something like, "What'd you say your major is? When exactly are you graduating?" Eventually, one guy actually called his buddy across town and introduced me over the phone. "You may want to meet this kid," he said. My contact didn't have anything open, but he knew that his friend, Bill Ellinger, was looking for a young salesperson. Bill took a shot on me. Two weeks after graduating from Dickinson College, I was working in market research and sales for Butcher & Singer, a wonderful regional firm that launched my career in the investment business.

The point is, if you are a college student with a less-than-impressive résumé, don't be afraid to talk to people. Be yourself. Listen. Don't B.S. Think creatively. And always ask for advice; older people (like we are now) love that.

COPING WITH "BOOMERANG" CHILDREN

You made it! You got the kids through college, and you and your spouse are finally looking forward to some quality time alone together. What a great opportunity to plan for your retirement— or something even more romantic. As comedian Billy Crystal noted after his daughters left the nest, now you can walk around naked in your own house again.

Not so fast! A recent survey conducted by jobtrak.com, an online job service for students, found that 60 percent of college kids plan to live with their parents after graduation. About one-fourth plan to live with Mom and Dad for more than a year. For a lot of aging boomers, that bathroom door will need to stay closed for a while longer.

"Boomerang" children is the phrase used to describe the grown kids of boomers who return home to live with parents after graduation. Statistics show that the phenomenon of children returning to the nest is rising. According to the National Survey of Households and Families, 10 percent of kids over twenty-five now live with their parents. Experts cite a convergence of factors responsible for this new demographic:

- **Debt.** College students are now graduating with a diploma *and* the aforementioned piles of debt. Besides student loans, credit card debt is rampant among grads. Estimates vary, but we regularly see recent graduates carrying unpaid credit card balances approaching $10,000.

- **Tight job market.** A college degree may well be required for success these days, but that doesn't mean a diploma guarantees a job offer.

- **High rent.** Real estate prices have risen dramatically, especially in the major metropolitan areas favored by many grads. The choice for many is to share a tiny apartment with two or three strangers, or live more affordably—and comfortably—at home.

- **New expenses.** No longer able to take advantage of college housing, food, and activities, recent graduates learn fast how expensive it is to live. Even with a decent salary, many first-year workers are astonished how little they actually have left over after paying taxes, insurance, and, of course, making debt payments.

- **Personal reasons.** Coming home can be a safe alternative if your child is coming off a failed relationship, illness, or other personal challenge.

Some parents welcome having an older kid around the house; others are not so sure. Either way, it's a safe bet that tensions will rise from time to time. If you agree to let your grown child live at home, sit down and have a frank discussion about expectations, financial and otherwise. Here are some guidelines:

- **Establish ground rules.** Both parents and college graduates crave independence. To avoid resentment, work together to create a list of fair objectives and goals. That could include "visiting hours" for friends, privacy time, quiet time, meal schedules, and so on.

- **Charge rent—and more.** Adult children who are not disabled should contribute to household expenses, and not just the mortgage or rent payment. Having another person in the house will increase utility bills, grocery bills, auto expenses—you name it. Paying rent is also a great motivator to find work.

- **Agree to a time limit.** How long is up to you, but by limiting your potential time together under the same roof, neither "guest" nor "landlord" will suffer from the "how-long-is-this-going-to-last" syndrome. When your time is up, you can always renew, if both parties agree.

- **Set the labor law.** If your recent graduate is out of work, create a set of paying jobs around the house. Some families simply deduct income earned from the child's rent. By performing chores like cooking, cleaning, yard work, and household repairs, your child will feel less like a charity case, your own workload will be lessened, and resentments won't get a chance to build. This could be the perfect opportunity for a kid to learn how to cook something other than macaroni and cheese!

Having grown-up kids around the house can provoke so many mixed emotions. For most of us, raising children is the greatest satisfaction of our lives—and yet we long to move on from that task. Taking the time early in life to teach your kids good financial habits will encourage them to be self-sufficient, and set an example of how to live. Grown-up kids who observe parents in control of their money, and not stressed out about the bills, will get the message that they can do it, too. That, more than money itself, should be your true legacy.

Chapter Ten:

Taking Care of Your Aging Parents

R ichard, Jane, and their three boys enjoy a typical middle-class lifestyle in a nice midwestern suburb where the couple grew up. Like many boomers in their late forties, they are trying hard to plan for the future; Richard maxes out his 401(k), they put $8,000 annually into a conventional IRA, and they fund a 529 account for their kids' college. Saving for the future and paying the current bills is a monthly juggling act that would seem familiar to many families. If only that were the whole story.

Richard's father died in 1999, leaving his ailing wife and a lot of loose financial ends. Sadly, Richard's only sibling, a sister, had died of brain cancer, leaving Richard (and of course Jane) alone to take care of Mom, now eighty-one. Things went downhill fast. "After Dad died," says Richard, "Mom went through two separate back surgeries and got diagnosed with breast cancer, plus had a litany of other health issues. I wanted to let her stay in her house as long as possible; she loves the place, and it's also five minutes away from us. Moving her out would be a big emotional issue for all of us, because it's also where I grew up. So we tried everything, including the 'Help! I've fallen and I can't get up!' necklace. She ultimately did fall, and dislocated her shoulder."

Richard goes on: "Making that final trip to the assisted-living facility was not fun. We had toured it to show her what it was like—very cute and charming, not dark and dreary. It was like a hotel. When we got there they gave us a temporary room, and as Jane and I were getting ready to leave, Mom sat in a chair and started to weep. I knelt down and held her hand and said, 'Don't worry, Mom, everything's gonna be fine. They have great food, you'll meet new friends, there are lots of things to do.'

"That's when it hit me. In the back of my mind, I could hear my mother saying the same things to me when she dropped me off at summer camp, thirty years ago. Talk about the circle of life."

Here then is the last "slice" of the Sandwich Generation—caring for our parents. The same medical advances that will keep us humming for decades after retirement are also giving our parents many extra years. In the best of times, those years are filled with the joy of family gatherings, the attention of grandchildren, and fond memories of a life well lived. Yet for many elderly Americans and their families, old age is a time of stress and uncertainty. Questions of mortality and quality of life are no longer theoretical, and we face choices that did not even exist a few generations ago. An older parent unable to live alone and care for herself might well wonder if modern medicine is doing her a favor or robbing her of dignity. Complicating the emotions is the worry that her kids are being inconvenienced by her needs. Indeed, many grown children, already stressed about their own retirement plans and shouldering massive college bills for their own kids, wonder how they can cope with a parent who is too frail to care for herself but is not ready to die.

Richard puts it directly: "Taking my mother to the bathroom, pulling down her underwear, putting her on the toilet—psychologically, you do that stuff enough and it can get to you. It takes a huge emotional toll."

It can be especially hard when spouses find themselves taking care of in-laws. "My wife's been a saint," says Richard. "Jane and my mom do not always get along, but she's been carrying her around to doctor's appointments, trying to be a good daughter-in-law. We wear lots of different hats."

Not surprisingly, feelings of inadequacy and guilt are often part of the parental-care equation. And looming over it all is the huge expense of long-term care. When money enters the picture, you can be sure emotions will run high. This chapter addresses the financial aspects of caring for parents—but as you've learned throughout this book, good planning and honest discussions about money transcend mere dollars and cents. The *real* goal is the peace of mind, for yourself and your parents, that comes from knowing where you stand.

THE PARENT TRAP

You don't have to look far to find stressed-out families taking care of parents. A recent study based on a 2002 Canadian government survey found that 30 percent of citizens aged forty-five to sixty-four with children living at home were also taking care of a senior—typically a parent. Forty percent of those said the caregiving added expenses to the family budget. Of the 80 percent

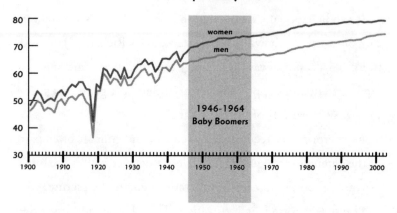

Life expectancy at birth

Source: CDC National Vital Statistics Report, Volume 53, Number 6.

who also worked for a living, 20 percent said that caring for the senior necessitated changes in their work schedule. Fifteen percent had to reduce their work hours, and 10 percent reported losing income. Half of all so-called intensive caregivers—defined in the study as those providing more than eight hours of care per month—reported changes in social activities.

Did we mention stress? Seventy percent of these sandwiched boomers reported feeling stressed, versus 61 percent of workers who were not caring for seniors and kids. From what we see from clients and callers every day, this is a very real issue!

David: Elder care is like a looming, dark cloud that's sneaking up on more and more of us. We know it's over our shoulder, and we want to be able to help our parents, but we're not sure how to approach it. There's a lot of fear and anxiety out there.

Jonathan: And no wonder. The cost of long-term care has risen 8 percent annually since 2002—that's more than twice the rate of inflation! Nationwide, the average annual cost of a nursing home is about $70,000 according to MetLife, although the price varies widely depending on where you live. In expensive regions of the country like the Northeast, nursing homes could easily cost double that. And most of us are in denial: a study by the Kaiser Family Foundation showed that six in ten Americans believe a nursing home costs less than $60,000 a year. Wrong!

David: Assisted-living facilities, which combine independence with professional care in a less institutional environment, can be cheaper. But it's hard to get a handle on assisted-living prices because, like hotels, the level of service and amenities is so varied. Some luxury assisted-living units can cost far more than a nursing home; you're buying a condo on the golf course, with round-the-clock care included. Take a guess at what that costs! It's also difficult to comparison shop because facilities have different fee structures. One place might include the cost of daily pill-taking reminders, while another adds that service onto the bill as an à la carte charge.

Jonathan: Prices are all over the map, but one thing is certain: *Medicare won't pay for any of it!* (Except for certain short-term nursing-home stays after hospitalization.) That often surprises people, who possibly confuse Medicare, which we all get at age sixty-five, with Medicaid—a state-and-federal partnership to provide health care for low-income families, including seniors. (More on Medicare options later in this chapter.) If your parent qualifies in your state, Medicaid *does* pay for very basic, possibly even grim, nursing-home care. (There will be no golf course.) But, like welfare, it's hardly something to look forward to, much less build into your financial plan. Medicaid nursing homes are for people who have no other options and have made no other plans. That should not be you, nor your parents.

IT TAKES A TEAM

Okay, the ticket to parent care is expensive, no matter how you ride. So where does the money come from? Earlier in this book we exhorted you to budget for rainy days, stop using credit cards, save for your retirement, and plan for your kids' college. Now we're saying you have to cough up gazillions more to keep your mom happy in a nursing home. "Uncle!" we hear from the chorus. "We're tapped out!"

The good news here is, caring for parents is usually not a solo job. You might have siblings and other relatives who can help—financially or otherwise. And, in many cases, your parents themselves will have some means. Look at this as a team effort, and it won't seem as onerous. Remember our government employees, Sandy and Carl? Sandy's parents are in an assisted living facility that costs $3,000 to $5,000 a month, depending on the level of service. "My mom is eighty-six and has dementia," says Sandy, "and my ninety-one-year-old dad can't take care of her. For a while, my sister and I were doing it all—taking time off from work, using up vacations; it was stressful. Assisted living has made a huge difference. Someone comes in and gets her moving in the morning, gets her cleaned up, then they do activities all day. My sister and I would never have enough time for all that, and my parents love it."

Right now, Sandy's parents are covering their own long-term

(continued on p. 290)

Talking Money with Mom and Dad

It's never easy to talk about money with your parents—especially when the money you're talking about is theirs. After all, they were in charge for so long, and now it's up to you. If you grew up in a family where money was never discussed in front of the kids, these conversations can even feel embarrassing—as if the subject were too private for words. In such situations, keep in mind that you are trying to help your parents, not invade their privacy. Think of the professional, businesslike way that a doctor examines you. In the same way, it's usually best to be frank but positive when working through financial issues with your parents.

- **It's about independence.** Rather than focusing immediately on the cost of this or that, make it clear right off the bat that you and your parents share the same interest: maintaining their independence. We've found that's the number-one goal of elderly people, and their kids. Listen to what matters most in their lives, like being able to shop for groceries, or attend clubs or concerts, and make it clear that you understand those needs. Just knowing you "get it" will put them at ease.

- **Help them to help themselves.** Many older parents shun the advice of their children, out of either pride or the worry that they will be a nuisance. In such cases it's often best to let them feel like the solutions are their own. This comes from careful listening and quiet empathy, even when you are sure you "know" the best path.

- **We're all going to die, but that's not the point.** Your parents know they're going to die, and probably sooner than you. They don't need to be reminded of it. They *do* need to hear how you can help them live in dignity. When discussing issues like advance health care directives, make it clear that the goal is improving their life, not planning for their death.

- **Talk about their legacy, not their will.** Even if your parents don't have much net worth, the subject of their will is bound to come up at some point. Even seniors of modest means usually have a home and personal property. It's possible that you or a sibling will be asked by your parents to be the executor of their estate. But conversations about wills and trusts don't

(continued on next page)

(from previous page)

have to dwell on death. Talk to your parents about how any inheritance might be used to further their legacy—such as paying for a grandchild's education, or simply building a nest egg for your own retirement and eventual legacy.

- **Lead by example.** It's hard to say what's worse: being lectured by your parents or being lectured by your kids. Either way, it rarely works. Just as you try to teach your children by your own example, you can make financial suggestions to your parents that are based on what has worked for you. For example, if you suspect your parents are living beyond their means and overusing credit cards (an increasingly common problem for seniors), show them how you manage your own money. Help them draw up a budget. "This worked for me, and it might work for you" is a nonjudgmental way to offer financial advice.

- **It takes a team.** Don't forget that elder care is a job for everyone in the family—siblings, your own children, and other relatives, not to mention your parents themselves. Family meetings are a great way to involve everyone and come up with constructive solutions.

Do *not* try to have this meeting on a major holiday or anniversary, which is already freighted with all sorts of expectations and obligations. Instead, schedule a "retreat" for some non-holiday weekend. Make it like a reunion or a picnic (with your parents as the guests of honor), but make it clear that serious business will also take place.

- **Be honest about your own financial concerns.** If you're worried about how you can afford elder care, discuss the issue calmly, after you've created an atmosphere of trust. Going forward, it won't help if you're feeling resentful or unappreciated.

By working together, you and your parents can solve a lot of financial problems, and feel better about yourselves in the process. Remember those stressed-out sandwiched boomers in the Canadian study? Despite their hectic schedules and multiple obligations, *95 percent said they felt satisfied with life!* At the end of the day, there *is* something deeply satisfying about caring for a parent. The circle of life that Richard observed is very real.

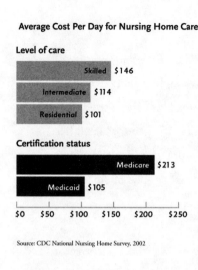

Average Cost Per Day for Nursing Home Care

Level of care

Skilled $146
Intermediate $114
Residential $101

Certification status

Medicare $213
Medicaid $105

$0 $50 $100 $150 $200 $250

Source: CDC National Nursing Home Survey, 2002

care with income from pensions (about $30,000 a year), Social Security, and modest savings of about $100,000. The savings won't last long, and Sandy knows that if her mother's condition deteriorates she will have to move to a nursing home, at a cost of $6,000 to $8,000 a month—way more than her parents' income. "At that point my sister and I may need to take out a loan to help them," says Sandy, "and we're prepared to do that." But given their ages, she adds, "I can't imagine this will go on too long."

Sandy's family could have avoided a lot of financial stress and uncertainty had her parents taken out a long-term care insurance policy when they were younger. (More on that below.) But they are mitigating the problems by working together and having frank talks about money.

PLANNING AHEAD WITH LONG-TERM CARE INSURANCE

By far the best way to prepare for elder care is through long-term care (LTC) insurance, an increasingly popular form of coverage.

LTC policies make up for a big gap in health care coverage, because normal health insurance (including, as we mentioned, Medicare) does not cover the huge cost of a nursing home or assisted living facility.

Jonathan: There is a catch to LTC coverage: it's quite expensive, reflecting the fact that about half of all people over sixty-five will need long-term care someday. Those are steep odds, and the premiums reflect the companies' risk.

David: As with life insurance, the younger you are, the cheaper the policy. Then again, the younger you are, the longer you'll presumably be paying. (If you stop making premium payments, your coverage ends and you will get no benefits later—and all your previous payments will have been wasted.) Let's take a closer look at LTC insurance, for your parents and yourself.

Who Needs It?

As we mentioned, about half of us will someday need long-term care. Those are much greater chances than a fire burning down your home, yet everyone has fire insurance. So you could argue that everyone should definitely have LTC coverage—including you and your parents. Most people don't, partly because they don't understand it and partly because of the expense, even though the premiums will cost much less than a nursing home. In 2005, the average cost of an LTC policy was about $2,000 a year. Of Americans aged forty-five to sixty-four who earn more than $20,000 a year, only 5 percent have LTC coverage. But most people *should* buy LTC coverage, starting sometime in their late fifties. We don't think it's wise to buy these policies any earlier, for two reasons:

- You could die before you need it, and the money will have been wasted. By the time you're approaching sixty, the chances have increased that you'll need long-term care someday.

- Your combined premiums, over decades of your life, could outweigh the benefit. Until you're nearing sixty, you're better off investing that money for retirement.

Waiting until you're much older than sixty will get very expensive on an annual basis, but it could still work out very much in your favor. For example, let's say Jonathan buys a policy at age fifty-five that costs $2,000 a year. David buys the same coverage, but because he waits until he's seventy, he pays big-time: $5,000 a year. Both twins enter a nursing home at age eighty. At that point, each will have paid exactly the same in total premiums—$50,000. (Jonathan paid $2,000 a year for twenty-five years, and David paid $5,000 a year for ten years.)

That's a lot of money—but in both cases, the total paid is far less than the cost of even *one year* in a nursing home.

So why not just wait until you're seventy, or later, to buy LTC insurance? For starters, you don't know how old you'll be when you need long-term care. Like all insurance, with LTC policies if you wait to buy coverage until you need it, it's too late. Secondly, most policies require a fairly rigorous physical exam, to make sure that you're not already knocking on the door of the nursing home. Wait too long, and your health could disqualify you.

Let's go back to Richard and his ailing mother. In 2000, a year after her husband died and when she was seventy-six, Richard's mother (at his suggestion) took out an LTC policy through GE Capital, one of many LTC insurers. At her age, the cost was a whopping $11,000 a year, but Richard sensed it was a good idea. "I was trying to protect my father's estate," he explains. "It's not a huge pot of money—about half a million bucks—but I didn't want to see it drained on nursing home care." His mother passed the physical. One month later, she was diagnosed with breast cancer. "We got in by the skin of our teeth," he says.

Richard's mother paid premiums for four-and-a-half years, or about $50,000, before entering the assisted living facility. (Premiums stop when care begins.) Her care costs $4,700 a month, of which GE Capital pays $4,300. Annual benefit: $51,600. "Basically, the policy paid for itself in one year of assisted living," says Richard.

It's hard to see the downside in buying an LTC policy. Some people calculate they could do better by investing all that premium money, which of course is what the insurance company

(continued on p. 298)

How to Shop for LTC Insurance

Prices for LTC insurance vary widely, and it can be hard to comparison shop because the details of policies are so different. Here are some of the basic terms you'll need to know, with some advice on what to look for.

The **daily benefit** is how much the insurance company will pay for each day of care. It sounds simple, but look closely. If someone is receiving home health care (a growing trend), she might have several caregivers on one day, then several days go by with no or limited care. The result is that the care on the "busy" days could exceed the daily financial limit—even though the overall care for that week would be within the total allowed for seven days. To get around this problem, look for policies that calculate benefits based on a *weekly or monthly maximum*, not a strict day-to-day tally. The best policies go even further and simply project your daily benefit over the benefit period you have bought (see below), then guarantee that total *pool of money*—regardless of how much is spent each day or month.

However it's calculated, a larger daily benefit will obviously mean a more expensive policy. When calculating what you'll need, consider that the average daily rate for a private room in a nursing home is now about $200. But because care costs vary so widely across the country, you should research facilities in the community where the care will likely be given. You can get detailed information about the cost of nursing homes, assisted-living centers, and home health care all over the country from MetLife's Mature Market Institute (www.maturemarketinstitute.com).

The **benefit period** refers to the duration of the stay that is covered. This can range from a few years to forever, with concurrent increases in premium cost. The average nursing-home stay is between four and five years, but patients with Alzheimer's often stay for much longer. We recommend buying a six-year policy; longer stays are unlikely, but if it makes you more comfortable and your budget can handle it, you could buy a lifetime policy. Whatever the benefit period, be sure to get a policy with a *restoration of benefits* clause, which means that if the patient gets better and leaves the facility (or stops needing home care), he can start paying premiums again and reset the clock for another complete benefit period in the future.

The **elimination period** is essentially a deductible—the period of time up front for which you'll have to pay yourself. Elimination periods of thirty to ninety days are common, but unless you can easily afford a month or two in a nursing home, we think it's better to pay a slightly higher premium and get an even shorter elimination period, or none at all. Note that when tallying the elimination period, some companies count only *service days* (bad) versus *calendar days* (good). Either way, the elimination period should only apply to the first stay or home care visit; subsequent stays should be covered from day one.

Inflation protection is an essential rider given the ballooning cost of health care. Your policy won't do you much good if, by the time you or your parent needs it, the coverage doesn't even pay for basics. Inflation protection is calculated a number of ways; we prefer policies that offer a 5 percent annual increase, compounded.

(continued on next page)

(from previous page)

Even that won't keep up with current runaway health care costs, so you may need to plan on contributing some of your own money. But note that policies sold to seniors over age seventy-five probably don't need so much inflation protection. In that case, a plan with periodic inflation adjustments would suffice.

Guaranteed renewable means the company can't cancel a policy, even if it stops selling LTC insurance. That's important, because obviously this type of coverage is meant to protect people far into the future. It's also wise to get a policy in which the premium can't be increased, except for across-the-board raises to all policyholders.

Read carefully the sections of the policy dealing with **level of service**, which can make all the difference. The best policies cover nursing homes, assisted-living facilities, and home health agency care. Avoid policies that require a hospital stay before coverage kicks in. Also pay attention to the medical conditions that must be met before the company will pay; one policy could define "ability to eat" very differently than that of another company. "You really have to read the fine print," advises Richard. "One thing I never thought about is what happens when my mom has to leave the assisted-living center for hospital treatment. We have to keep paying for her room at the center, but the insurance won't reimburse us if she's gone more than fifty days in a calendar year. It's not like I can say, 'Sorry, Mom, you can't get your knee replaced because you've got to stay in your room.' But I've got to keep track of it all; the onus is on us to essentially prove she was there every day."

The majority of LTC policies are **tax-qualified**, which means the policyholder can deduct premiums from income tax as a health care expense. (You still need all health care expenses to exceed 7.5 percent of your adjusted gross income in order to claim a deduction.) In addition, the benefits from tax-qualified plans are not taxed as income. Under tax-qualified plans, a doctor must certify that the patient is either *cognitively impaired* or is unable to perform at least two of the six *activities of daily living*: eating, bathing, dressing, using a toilet, transferring from a bed to a chair, and maintaining continence.

The latest trend in LTC insurance is **limited-pay policies**, which involve forking over a single lump sum premium in return for coverage. (Some limited-pay policies spread the premium out over several payments, or end premiums at age sixty-five.) These can be a good deal if you have the cash, because you never have to worry about rate hikes. Wealthy individuals can use these policies to buy LTC insurance for their own children, in the process reducing their estate tax liability.

More than one hundred companies are selling LTC insurance, so it pays to shop around. A good local agent can help guide you through the maze. Perhaps more than any other type of insurance, your LTC policy should be locked in with a well-established, national player that's committed to the business. Avoid "newbies" or regional underwriters that have only been selling LTC insurance for a few years. The safest bet is to pick insurance companies with an A+ or better rating from A.M. Best. (Get free ratings at www.ambest.com.)

LTC insurance isn't the only way to pay for extended care. Other options to consider are reverse mortgages and annuities, which were explained in Chapter Seven.

does with it. But with the rising cost of long-term care, you'd have to count on historically high returns to make that work to your advantage. To take our earlier example, if Jonathan had instead invested his $2,000 annual premium in the stock market for twenty-five years, and if the market averaged 10 percent annually, he'd enter the nursing home with a little more than $200,000. Assuming average inflation, that might pay for one year of care by that time. Of course, if Jonathan is one of the half of us who won't ever need long-term care, he looks smart: he's sitting on $200,000. But is that a chance most people should take? We don't think so.

That said, there are situations where it might not be advisable to buy LTC insurance. Obviously if you are barely scraping by even while living within your means, LTC insurance could be a tough burden. The biggest danger is that you will pay premiums for years, then hit a rough patch in your financial life and be forced to cancel the policy before using it. What a waste! If you think there is any chance you might not be able to make the payments down the road, LTC insurance is not for you.

THE MEDICARE MAZE

Americans are pretty much on their own when it comes to figuring out a secure, comfortable retirement. But one aspect of old age does have a substantial backstop: basic health care. Millions of Americans got a crash course in Medicare (and its shortfalls!) with the introduction of the Part D prescription drug program in 2006. For all its failings, the plan did serve as a wakeup call to boomers that we need to understand our government-sponsored health benefits—for our parents' sake as well as our own. So before leaving the subject of parental care, let's take a look at what's currently out there in terms of government support. For more information, go to www.medicare.gov.

Medicare A

This is half of the original Medicare plan, and it covers hospital stays for anyone age sixty-five or older. It also covers limited stays in nursing homes and some home health agency care. You must meet deductibles for all benefit periods, and hospital stays are limited to sixty days, at which point steep co-payments start to kick in.

Medicare B

Part B represents the other half of the original Medicare plan. It covers 80 percent of most doctor visits, lab fees, outpatient hospital services, and medical equipment. It's not free, but the monthly premiums are dirt cheap compared to private health insurance, and they can be deducted from your Social Security check. Not all doctors will accept Medicare patients because in some cases they consider the government payments to be too low.

Medigap

This is private insurance that makes up the "gap" in Medicare coverage—such as paying your 20-percent coinsurance and other charges not covered. Medigap plans are sold in ten categories labeled A through J, with A being the least comprehensive and J providing the most coverage. The most popular plan is Medigap C, which pays (among other things) for Part A hospital deductibles and Part B deductibles and coinsurance. Because Medigap is sold by private companies, rates vary considerably. The good news is, everybody's plans provide exactly the same coverage in each category, so it's easy to comparison shop.

Medicare C

Also known as managed-care plans, these are the Medicare version of HMOs. They're essentially government-subsidized, private alternatives to Medicare—but you need to be enrolled in Medicare B (and make those payments) to qualify. In return, you'll get additional benefits, often including drug plans, at a higher premium cost. (You can switch back to Medicare B if you don't like the plan.) Generally these are a better deal then Medigap coverage.

Medicare D

The new prescription drug plan is still on a rocky shakedown cruise at this writing, and it remains to be seen what changes are in store. Like Medicare C, the plan involves a subsidized but largely private-market drug benefit, with many different options. One major complaint has been the difficulty in determining which plan is right for which senior, because not all plans cover all drugs equally. So the right choice depends in large part on what your medications are—or might be down the road. That's not easy! Complicating matters is the fact that every state has an array of different plans. One complaint we've heard a lot is that it's hard for boomers who live in one state to help their parents (who live in another state) sort through the plans. Not surprisingly, many seniors with Medicare C private drug plans are staying put until the dust settles.

It's understandable if you (or your parents) are overwhelmed with all of these options concerning Medicare coverage and prescription drugs. In fact, it may be metaphorical for this entire chapter on our aging parents and money: so many options to choose from—where to live, what to do, how to pay for it all. Here's the thing to remember, though: unlike saving for our retirement or our children's education, caring for our parents is primarily our parents' job. Sure, we want to provide for them if they need help. Of course we should be there to support them if they need it. But let's not forget, first, that we have other obligations to attend to (like ensuring that we don't become dependent on *our* children), and second, that our parents probably don't *want* us taking control of their lives. We could write another entire book on the pitfalls and shortcomings of Social Security and Medicare. But you know what? At least it's *something*. At least we have that stopgap, as imperfect—and under construction—as it is.

It's strange: when we bring up this topic of "money and parents" with the parents themselves, they don't want our money; they want our time—and our kids' time. That's what they really want. So if you want to help your folks as they become older and more frail, see them more often. Turn your cell phone off, put a fresh pot of coffee on, and hang out on that old family sofa. Through old-fashioned "talking," you can discover the financial and logistical solutions that suit your entire family the best. It probably won't be a perfect solution, but if you're spending time visiting with your parents, chances are they won't want to be anywhere else. You're there if they need you; you're there when they don't. That, in essence, is what family, and this chapter, is all about.

Chapter Eleven:

It's About Your Life

t usually begins with the numbers. But that's rarely where it ends. When new clients come to see us for financial advice: they're frustrated with their current advisor, they need to set up a college savings plan, they have proceeds from a divorce or inheritance, they want to know what to do with their 401(k), they need a loan, etc. Then, almost invariably, it gets personal. Because as people describe their financial picture, they begin to describe their lives. And once they feel comfortable enough to share the details, the conversation morphs into something more like a counseling session, because, in many cases, these are things they haven't discussed with *anyone* before.

One of the issues people in our generation want to get off

their chest is how difficult it is. Okay, okay—so we didn't live through the Great Depression, or save the world from tyranny. But we have our own crosses to bear: do-it-yourself retirements where nothing is certain, kids attending colleges that drain our savings, parents needing basic care that costs more than our house. Now, once again, our generation is inventing solutions as we go along.

Let's face it—money is about much more than *money*. This subject is an intimate one. Tears are quite common in our business. As we talk with clients about the important issues that lurk *behind* the money—things like dreams, aspirations, fears, and frustrations—it's clear what this is all about.

It's really all about your life, and how you want to live it. If you believe that, our job as financial advisors becomes straightforward: to help you clarify and visualize your destination . . . then give you the tools you'll need to get there.

Seen this way, financial planning isn't a burden; it's liberating! This is an important distinction, because the only way to really master your money—to move beyond the syndrome of lurching from one financial crisis to the next—is through daily practice. We don't want to make it sound like finance is a twelve-step program, but the fact is, good money management happens one day at a time. Unfortunately, we've seen too often that if you approach your finances like a nagging chore, you'll eventually drop out, give up, and go back to old habits. But if you see this as something bigger, about replacing fears and frustrations with a very real transformation, you'll keep it up for life with the enthusiasm of the converted.

How does daily financial practice work? Well, if you think back on the structure of this book, it starts with getting organized. Sorting through mail, filing important papers, and staying on top of bills is a daily practice. Likewise, keeping track of your spending, and always looking out for better deals, just becomes a daily habit for the financially fit.

This doesn't mean you have to walk around constantly obsessing over money. It's more the opposite: by making money management a small part of your daily ritual, you won't have to worry about it all the time. The money will begin to take care of itself.

Throughout this book we've stressed the importance of planning and preparation—whether it's preparing for your retirement, your kids' college, your parents' care, or your next vacation. The image we keep coming back to is a garden. (All those years we spent with rakes in our hands weren't for nothing!) Gardening can be a deeply satisfying pursuit, and a great way to learn patience, because nothing dramatic in a garden happens overnight. It's the same with money, which grows incredibly over time but rarely changes much in a month or two.

Preparation, which is the opposite of instant gratification, makes it possible to weather life's inevitable surprises. That means more than just having an emergency savings fund, although that's an important early step to financial fitness. In a larger, more cosmic sense, it means being mentally and emotionally prepared for adversity. And, again, the way you reach that level of preparedness is by daily "exercise." We have seen how people in control of their money in a sensible way actually sleep better at night, and have better relationships with their spouse, their children, and their colleagues. And we have never met *anyone* who was sorry that they learned to live within their means, even when it meant short-term sacrifices.

As we mentioned in the beginning of this book, personal finance isn't about competing against anyone. It's about defining your own game of life and succeeding at that. And as you move into your new routine, you'll realize that it can be a very positive process. Fear dissipates. Anxiety lessens. You gain control of a part of your life that you very likely may not have had before. Each step reinforces the next: the plan, the process, the strategy, the execution. Do these things, and you—and the people you love—will be headed to financial peace of mind and, we hope, a life of happiness and fulfillment.

No, money doesn't buy that happiness. In fact, we introduced you to people we know who live quite happily without much money at all. It's not about how much money you have, it's how you handle it, how you make it work to help you attain the life you want, that counts. It's about realistic and thoughtful planning, not endless millions. And the great news is, it's not too late if you get started today. Tell yourself that today is a new beginning—a clean slate for you to pursue whatever it is that gives you fulfillment and meaning. Now is the time to make a difference.

It can be hard to phase out the noise all around us and focus on what really matters; sometimes life feels like a cell phone that never stops ringing. No wonder so many boomers are searching for ways to reduce stress. It might seem strange to say this, but personal finance has its own spiritual dimension. Accepting what you have, living responsibly within your means, facing adversity with both a calm strength and a constructive, solution-oriented approach—these are all principles of a balanced life, not just a balanced checkbook. Maybe we can't turn back the clock to the simpler life of our parents and grandparents, but we *can* simplify our *outlook,* starting with the way we handle money. It always begins with the numbers. By going forward in confidence and knowing our goals, we can do this. We can go home again.